Django 4 for the Impatient

Learn the core concepts of Python web development with Django in one weekend

Greg Lim

Daniel Correa

BIRMINGHAM—MUMBAI

Django 4 for the Impatient

Copyright © 2022 Packt Publishing

Associate Group Product Manager: Pavan Ramchandani

Publishing Product Manager: Bhavya Rao

Senior Editor: Mark Dsouza

Content Development Editor: Divya Vijayan

Technical Editor: Saurabh Kadave

Copy Editor: Safis Editing

Project Coordinator: Ajesh Devavaram

Proofreader: Safis Editing

Indexer: Tejal Daruwale Soni

Production Designer: Vijay Kamble

Marketing Coordinator: Anamika Singh and Marylou De Mello

First published: June 2022

Production reference: 1170622

Published by Packt Publishing Ltd.
Livery Place
35 Livery Street
Birmingham
B3 2PB, UK.

ISBN 978-1-80324-583-6

www.packt.com

To my awesome wife for taking such good care of our family and children that I could embark on my writing journey. She and our family are the very reason why I write books like this. Thank you so much, dear.

– Greg Lim

To my mother, my ultimate hero.

– Daniel Correa

Contributors

About the author

Greg Lim is a technologist and the author of several books on programming. He has taught programming in tertiary institutions for many years and places a strong emphasis on learning by doing. Follow Greg on Twitter at @greglim81

> *"I want to thank Daniel, my talented co-author; without him, this book wouldn't have been possible. Thanks also to everyone on the Packt team who helped us so much."*

Daniel Correa is a researcher, software developer, and author of programming books. He has a PhD in computer science. He is a professor at Universidad EAFIT in Colombia. He is interested in software architectures, frameworks (such as Laravel, Nest, Django, Express, Vue, React, and Angular), web development, and clean code. Follow Daniel on Twitter at @danielgarax

> *"I want to thank Greg for letting me be part of this project. Greg is one of the best programming book authors I have known. Thanks to my wife, family, colleagues, and friends for all the support. Finally, thanks to the entire Packt team for the meticulous work to publish this book."*

About the reviewer

Abdelrahman Mostafa is an Egyptian Python developer, YouTuber, and consultant at the SmartSystem company in IBM's Maximo product. He has more than 4 years of experience in the field of web development. He graduated from the Faculty of Computer Science at Assiut University. He has developed many websites for major companies using the Django framework. In his spare time, he likes to play sports, especially boxing and bodybuilding, and one of his hobbies is constantly learning new things.

> *"I'd like to thank my family and friends who understand the time and commitment it takes to review this book. I'd also like to thank my father, who helped me and taught me – may he rest in peace. I truly believe all of us in the technical world are standing on the shoulders of giants. The giants for me are my leaders, Eng Alaa Hassab, Eng Ahmed Gomaa, Eng Islam Yahya and more who have left a mark on my working life and helped me achieve my goal."*

Sai Vivek Annamneni is an Application developer who has worked in Fujitsu, Accenture for 4 years in various evolving technologies like Python, AWS, Django for many projects like web applications in various industries like stock market, insurance, and Ecom. Also, he's involved in problem solving algorithms.

By qualification, he has a Master's degree in the stream of Computer Science from River University, Nashua in United States. Actively working to Found a startup with multiple streams of services and Products in the STAFFING industry in USA.

Mahmoud Abou-Elnaga is a software engineer from Egypt working as a freelancer who has taken many courses and certificates such as the Advanced Django course offered by Duke University and many courses on Udemy.

Table of Contents

4
Generating HTML Pages with Templates

5
Working with Models

6
Displaying Objects from Admin

7
Understanding the Database

8

Extending Base Templates

9

Creating a Movie Detail Page

10

Implementing User Signup and Login

11

Letting Users Create, Read, Update, and Delete Movie Reviews

12

Deploying the Application to the Cloud

Index

Other Books You May Enjoy

Preface

Django is a free, open source web framework for building modern Python web applications.

This book will help you get up and running with the fundamentals of Django. You will start building your first Django app within minutes. The book provides you with short explanations and a practical approach that cover some of the most important Django features, including the Django apps' structure, URLs, views, templates, models, CSS inclusion, image storage, authentication and authorization, the Django admin panel, and much more.

You will develop a movie reviews application across the book chapters. The movie reviews application will be the means to understand straightforward and complex Django concepts and how Django features can be used to implement full-stack web applications.

By the end of this book, you will be able to develop your own Django web applications and deploy them to the cloud.

Who this book is for

This book is for Python developers at any level of experience with Python programming who want to build full-stack Python web applications using Django. The book is for absolute Django beginners.

What this book covers

Chapter 1, Installing Python and Django, introduces Django and explains how to install Python, pip, and Django.

Chapter 2, Understanding the Project Structure and Creating Our First App, discusses the Django project structure and shows how to create a movie reviews application with Django.

Chapter 3, Managing Django URLs, explains how to create custom pages and how Django URLs work.

Chapter 4, Generating HTML Pages with Templates, takes a look at Django templates and how to separate HTML code from Django views.

Chapter 5, Working with Models, discusses the fundamentals of Django models and how to work with databases.

Chapter 6, Displaying Objects from Admin, shows how to collect and display information stored in a database.

Chapter 7, Understanding the Database, shows how to inspect the database information and how to switch between database engines.

Chapter 8, Extending Base Templates, explores how Django base templates can be used to reduce duplicated code and improve the look and feel of the movie reviews application.

Chapter 9, Creating a Movie Detail Page, enhances the movie reviews application with a feature to navigate to each movie's detail page.

Chapter 10, Implementing User Signup and Login, discusses the Django authentication system and enhances the movie reviews application with some features to allow users to sign up and log in.

Chapter 11, Letting Users Create, Read, Update, and Delete Movie Reviews, enhances the movie reviews application with standard CRUD operations on reviews for movies.

Chapter 12, Deploying the Application to the Cloud, shows how to deploy Django applications on the cloud.

To get the most out of this book

You will need Python 3.8+ installed, pip, and a good code editor such as Visual Studio Code. The last chapter requires the use of Git to deploy the application code to the cloud. All the software requirements are available for Windows, macOS, and Linux.

Software/hardware covered in the book	Operating system requirements
Python 3.8+	Windows, macOS, or Linux
pip	Windows, macOS, or Linux
Visual Studio Code	Windows, macOS, or Linux
Git	Windows, macOS, or Linux

If you are using the digital version of this book, we advise you to type the code yourself or access the code from the book's GitHub repository (a link is available in the next section). Doing so will help you avoid any potential errors related to the copying and pasting of code.

Download the example code files

You can download the example code files for this book from GitHub at `https://github.com/PacktPublishing/Django-4-for-the-Impatient`. If there's an update to the code, it will be updated in the GitHub repository.

We also have other code bundles from our rich catalog of books and videos available at `https://github.com/PacktPublishing/`. Check them out!

Download the color images

We also provide a PDF file that has color images of the screenshots and diagrams used in this book. You can download it here: `https://static.packt-cdn.com/downloads/9781803245836_ColorImages.pdf`.

Conventions used

There are a number of text conventions used throughout this book.

`Code in text`: Indicates code words in text, database table names, folder names, filenames, file extensions, pathnames, dummy URLs, user input, and Twitter handles. Here is an example: " These apps are loaded in the `INSTALLED_APPS` variable in the `moviereviews/settings.py` file."

A block of code is set as follows:

```
MEDIA_ROOT = os.path.join(BASE_DIR,'media')
MEDIA_URL = '/media/'
```

When we wish to draw your attention to a particular part of a code block, the relevant lines or items are set in bold:

```
urlpatterns = [
    path('admin/', admin.site.urls),
    path('', movieViews.home),
    path('about/', movieViews.about),
```

```
        path('signup/', movieViews.signup, name='signup'),
]
```

Any command-line input or output is written as follows:

```
pip3 install Django==4.0
```

Bold: Indicates a new term, an important word, or words that you see onscreen. For instance, words in menus or dialog boxes appear in **bold**. Here is an example: " For Windows, you must select the **Add Python 3.* to PATH** option."

> **Tips or Important Notes**
> Appear like this.

Get in touch

Feedback from our readers is always welcome.

General feedback: If you have questions about any aspect of this book, email us at customercare@packtpub.com and mention the book title in the subject of your message.

Errata: Although we have taken every care to ensure the accuracy of our content, mistakes do happen. If you have found a mistake in this book, we would be grateful if you would report this to us. Please visit www.packtpub.com/support/errata and fill in the form.

Piracy: If you come across any illegal copies of our works in any form on the internet, we would be grateful if you would provide us with the location address or website name. Please contact us at copyright@packt.com with a link to the material.

If you are interested in becoming an author: If there is a topic that you have expertise in and you are interested in either writing or contributing to a book, please visit authors.packtpub.com.

Share Your Thoughts

Once you've read *Django 4 for the Impatient*, we'd love to hear your thoughts! Scan the QR code below to go straight to the Amazon review page for this book and share your feedback.

https://packt.link/r/1803245832

Your review is important to us and the tech community and will help us make sure we're delivering excellent quality content.

1
Installing Python and Django

Welcome to *Django 4 for the Impatient*! This book focuses on the key tasks and concepts to help you to learn and build **Django** applications fast. It is designed for readers who don't need all the details about Django except for concepts that you really need to know. By the end of this book, you will be confident creating your own Django projects.

So, what's Django? Django is a free, open source web framework for building modern **Python** web applications. Django helps you quickly build web apps by abstracting away many of the repetitive challenges involved in building a website, such as connecting to a database, handling security, enabling user authentication, creating URL routes, displaying content on a page through templates and forms, supporting multiple database backends, and setting up an admin interface.

This reduction in repetitive tasks allows developers to focus on building a web application's functionality rather than reinventing the wheel for standard web application functions.

Django is one of the most popular frameworks available and is used by established companies such as *Instagram*, *Pinterest*, *Mozilla*, and *National Geographic*. It is also easy enough to be used in start-ups and for building personal projects.

There are other popular frameworks, such as Flash in Python and Express in *JavaScript* (For more information on Express, see *Beginning Node.js, Express & MongoDB Development* by Greg Lim). But these frameworks only provide the minimum required functionality for a simple web page, and developers have to do more foundational work, such as installing and configuring third-party packages on their own for basic website functionality.

In this chapter, we are going to get acquainted with the application we are going to build using Django 4 and get ready for our project by installing and setting up everything we need. By the end of the chapter, you will have successfully created your development environment.

In this chapter, we will be covering the following topics:

- Understanding the app we will be building
- Installing Python
- Installing Django
- Running the Django local web server

Technical requirements

In this chapter, we will be using **Python 3.8+** and **pip**.

The code for this chapter is located at `https://github.com/PacktPublishing/Django-4-for-the-Impatient/tree/main/Chapter01/moviereviews`.

Understanding the app we will be building

For our project, we will be building a movie reviews app that will allow users to view and search for movies, as shown in *Figure 1.1*:

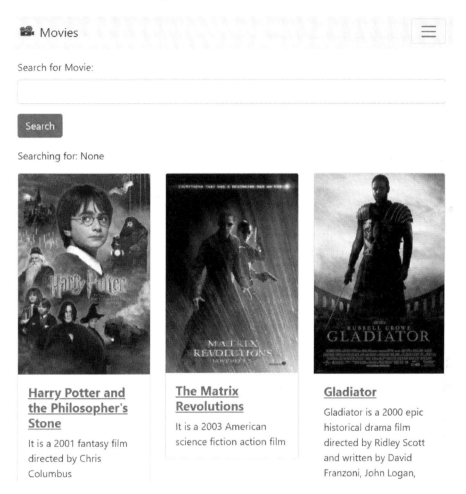

Figure 1.1 – A home page with search functionality

Users will also be able to log in and post reviews of any movies they may have watched, as shown in *Figure 1.2*:

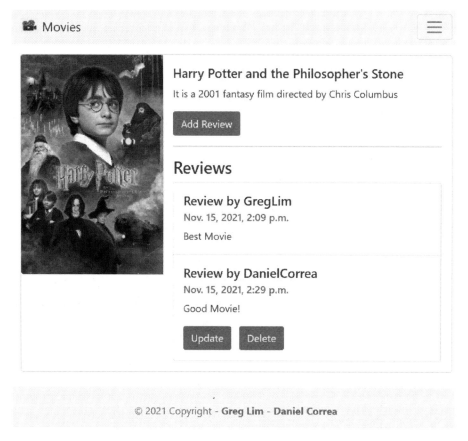

Figure 1.2 – A movie page listing reviews

They will be able to type in and add their review, as shown in *Figure 1.3*:

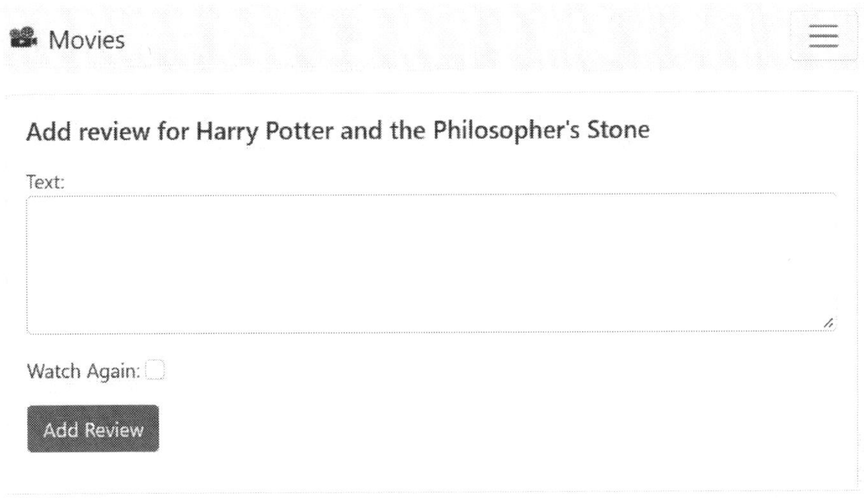

Figure 1.3 – An interface for writing a review

Users can see the list of reviews on a movie's page and post, edit, or delete their own review if they are logged in. They will not be able to edit or delete other users' reviews though. Through building this app, we will learn a lot of concepts, such as forms, user authorization, permissions, foreign keys, and more.

Let's begin by installing Python and Django.

Installing Python

First, let's check whether we have Python installed and, if so, what version we have.

If you are using a Mac, open your Terminal. If you are using Windows, open Command Prompt. For convenience, I will refer to both Terminal and Command Prompt as *Terminal* throughout the book.

We will need to check whether we have at least Python 3.8 in order to use Django 4. To do so, go to your Terminal and run the following commands.

For macOS, run this:

```
python3 --version
```

For Windows, run this:

```
python --version
```

This shows the version of Python you have installed. Make sure that the version is at least 3.8. If it isn't, get the latest version of Python by going to `https://www.python.org/downloads/` and installing the version for your OS. For Windows, you must select the **Add Python 3.* to PATH** option, as shown in *Figure 1.4*:

Figure 1.4 – Install Python on Windows

After the installation, run the command again to check the version of Python installed.

The output should reflect the latest version of Python, such as Python 3.10.2 (at the time of writing).

Installing Django

We will be using pip to install Django. pip is the standard package manager for Python to install and manage packages not part of the standard Python library. pip is automatically installed if you downloaded Python from `https://www.python.org/`.

First, check whether you have pip installed by going to the Terminal and running the following.

For macOS, run this:

```
pip3
```

For Windows, run this:

```
pip
```

If you have pip installed, the output should display a list of pip commands. To install Django, run the following command:

For macOS, run this:

```
pip3 install Django==4.0
```

For Windows, run this:

```
pip install Django==4.0
```

The preceding command will retrieve the latest Django code and install it on your machine. After installation, close and reopen your Terminal.

Ensure you have installed Django by running the following commands.

For macOS, run this:

```
python3 -m django
```

For Windows, run this:

```
python -m django
```

Now, the output will show you all the Django commands you can use, as shown in *Figure 1.5*:

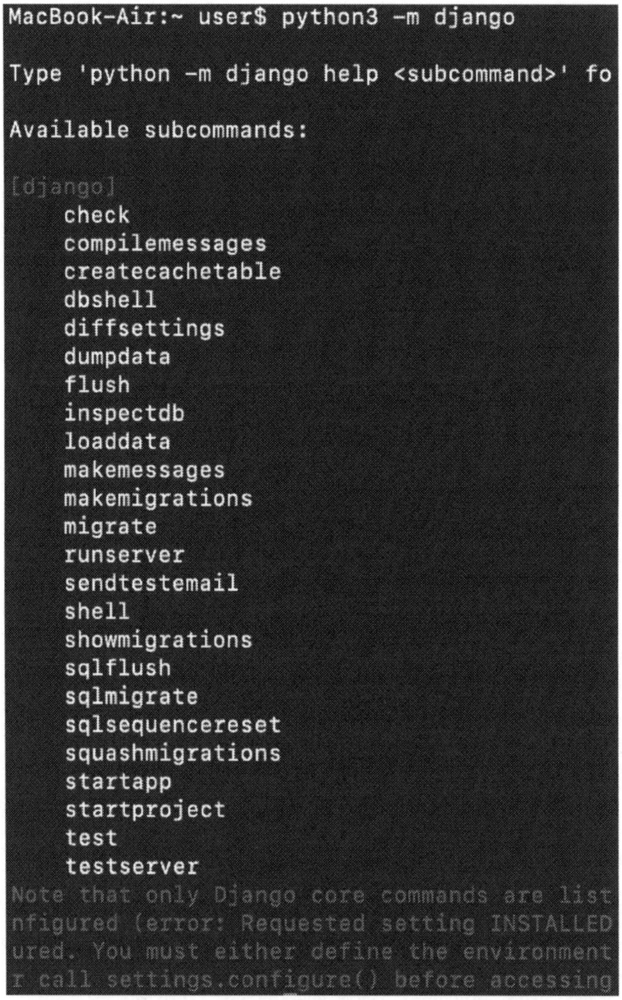

```
MacBook-Air:~ user$ python3 -m django

Type 'python -m django help <subcommand>' fo

Available subcommands:

[django]
    check
    compilemessages
    createcachetable
    dbshell
    diffsettings
    dumpdata
    flush
    inspectdb
    loaddata
    makemessages
    makemigrations
    migrate
    runserver
    sendtestemail
    shell
    showmigrations
    sqlflush
    sqlmigrate
    sqlsequencereset
    squashmigrations
    startapp
    startproject
    test
    testserver
Note that only Django core commands are list
nfigured (error: Requested setting INSTALLED
ured. You must either define the environment
r call settings.configure() before accessing
```

Figure 1.5 – Django module commands

Along the course of the book, you will progressively be introduced to some of the commands. For now, we will use the `startproject` option to create a new project.

In the Terminal, navigate to a folder on your computer where you want to store your Django project, such as `Desktop`. In that folder, you will run a command like this:

```
python3 -m django startproject <project_name>
```

In our case, let's say we want to name our project `moviereviews`. We can do so by running the following.

For macOS, run this:

```
python3 -m django startproject moviereviews
```

For Windows, run this:

```
python -m django startproject moviereviews
```

A `moviereviews` folder will be created. We will discuss its contents later. For now, let's run our first website on the Django local web server.

Running the Django local web server

In the Terminal, `cd` into the created folder:

```
cd moviereviews
```

Then, run the following.

For macOS, run this:

```
python3 manage.py runserver
```

For Windows, run this:

```
python manage.py runserver
```

When you do so, you start the local web server on your machine (for local development purposes). There will be a URL link: `http://127.0.0.1:8000/` (equivalent to `http://localhost:8000`). Open the link in a browser and you will see the default landing page, as shown in *Figure 1.6*:

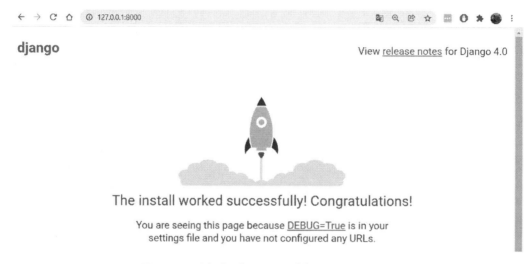

Figure 1.6 – The landing page of the Django project

This means that your local web server is running and serving the landing page. Sometimes, you will need to stop the server in order to run other Python commands. To stop the local server, press *Ctrl + C* in the Terminal.

Summary

In this chapter, you learned how to install and use Python, pip, and Django. You also learned how to create a new Django project and run a Django local web server. In the next chapter, we will look inside the project folder that Django has created for us to understand it better.

2
Understanding the Project Structure and Creating Our First App

Django projects contain a predefined structure with some key files. In this chapter, we will discuss the Django project structure and how some of those files are used to configure our web applications. Furthermore, Django projects are composed of one or more apps. We will learn how to create a movie app and how to register it inside our Django project.

In this chapter, we will cover the following topics:

- Understanding the project structure
- Creating our first app

Technical requirements

In this chapter, we will be using Python 3.8+. Additionally, we will be using the **Visual Studio (VS) Code** editor for building our web application in this book, which you can download from `https://code.visualstudio.com/`.

The code for this chapter is located at `https://github.com/PacktPublishing/Django-4-for-the-Impatient/tree/main/Chapter02/moviereviewsproject`.

Understanding the project structure

Let's look at the project files that were created for us in *Chapter 1*, *Installing Python and Django*, in the *Installing Django* section. Open the `moviereviews` project folder in VS Code. You will see the following elements:

Figure 2.1 – The MOVIEREVIEWS directory structure

Let's learn about each of these elements.

The moviereviews folder

As you can see in *Figure 2.1*, there is a folder with the same name as the folder we opened in VS Code originally – `moviereviews`. To avoid confusion and to distinguish between the two `moviereviews` folders, we will keep the inner `moviereviews` folder as it is and rename the outer folder `moviereviewsproject`.

After the renaming, open the inner `moviereviews` folder. You will see the following elements, as shown in *Figure 2.2*:

Figure 2.2 – The MOVIEREVIEWSPROJECT directory structure

Let's briefly look at all the elements in the `moviereviews` folder:

- `__pycache__`: This folder stores compiled bytecode when we generate our project. You can largely ignore this folder. Its purpose is to make your project start a little faster by caching the compiled code that can then be readily executed.

- `__init__.py`: This file specifies what to run when Django launches for the first time.

- `asgi.py`: This file allows an optional **Asynchronous Server Gateway Interface (ASGI)** to run.

- `settings.py`: The `settings.py` file is an important file that controls our project's settings. It contains several properties:

  - `BASE_DIR`: Determines where on your machine the project is situated.

  - `SECRET_KEY`: Used when you have data flowing in and out of your website. Do not ever share this with others.

- `DEBUG`: Our site can run in debug mode or not. In debug mode, we get detailed information on errors – for instance, if we try to run `http://localhost:8000/123` in the browser, we will see a **Page not found (404)** error:

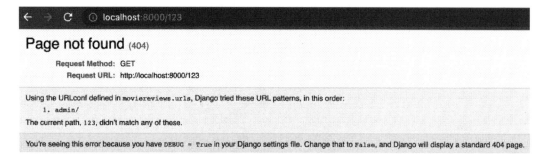

Figure 2.3 – Accessing an invalid application route

> **Note**
>
> It is important to remember the following:
>
> - When deploying our app to production, we should set `DEBUG` to `False`. If DEBUG = False, we will see a generic 404 page without error details.
>
> - While developing our project, we should set DEBUG = True to help us with debugging.

- `INSTALLED_APPS`: Allows us to bring different pieces of code into our project. We will see this in action later.

- `MIDDLEWARE`: Refers to built-in Django functions to process application requests/responses, which include authentication, session, and security.

- `ROOT_URLCONF`: Specifies where our URLs are.

- `TEMPLATES`: Defines the template engine class, the list of directories where the engine should look for template source files, and specific template settings.

- `AUTH_PASSWORD_VALIDATORS`: Allow us to specify the validations that we want on passwords – for example, a minimum length.

There are some other properties in `settings.py`, such as LANGUAGE_CODE and TIME_ZONE, but we have focused on the more important properties in the preceding list. We will later revisit this file and see how relevant it is in developing our site.

- `urls.py`: This file tells Django which pages to render in response to a browser or URL request. For example, when someone enters the `http://localhost:8000/123` URL, the request comes into `urls.py` and gets routed to a page based on the paths specified there. We will later add paths to this file and better understand how it works.

- `Wsgi.py`: This file stands for the **Web Server Gateway Interface** (**WSGI**) and helps Django serve our web pages. Both files are used when deploying our app. We will revisit them later when we deploy our app.

manage.py

The `manage.py` file seen in *Figure 2.1* and *Figure 2.2* is an element we should not tinker with. The file helps us to perform administrative operations. For example, we earlier ran the following command in *Chapter 1*, *Installing Python and Django*, in the *Running the Django local web server* section:

```
python3 manage.py runserver
```

The purpose of the command was to start the local web server. We will later illustrate more administrative functions, such as one for creating a new app – `python3 manage.py startapp`.

db.sqlite3

The `db.sqlite3` file contains our database. However, we will not discuss this file in this chapter, as we do not need it to create our file. We will do so in *Chapter 5*, *Working with Models*.

Let's next create our first app!

Creating our first app

A single Django project can contain one or more apps that work together to power a web application. Django uses the concept of projects and apps to keep code clean and readable.

For example, on a movie review site such as *Rotten Tomatoes*, as shown in *Figure 2.4*, we can have an app for listing movies, an app for listing news, an app for payments, an app for user authentication, and so on:

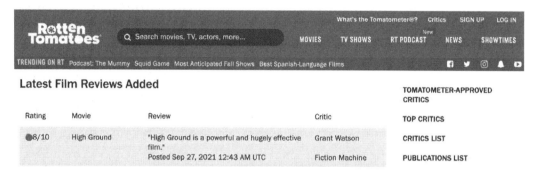

Figure 2.4 – The Rotten Tomatoes website

Apps in Django are like pieces of a website. You can create an entire website with one single app, but it is useful to break it up into different apps, each representing a clear function.

Our movie review site will begin with one app. We will later add more as we progress. To add an app, in the Terminal, stop the server by using *Cmd + C*. Navigate to the moviereviewsproject folder and run a command like the following in the Terminal:

```
python3 manage.py startapp <name of app>
```

In our case, we will add a movie app:

For macOS, run the following command:

```
python3 manage.py startapp movie
```

For Windows, run the following command:

```
python manage.py startapp movie
```

A new folder, movie, will be added to the project. As we progress in the book, we will explain the files that are inside the folder.

Although our new app exists in our Django project, Django doesn't recognize it till we explicitly add it. To do so, we need to specify it in settings.py. So, go to /moviereviews/settings.py, under INSTALLED_APPS, and you will see six built-in apps already there.

Add the app name, as highlighted in the following (this should be done whenever a new app is created):

```
...
INSTALLED_APPS = [
    'django.contrib.admin',
    'django.contrib.auth',
    'django.contrib.contenttypes',
    'django.contrib.sessions',
    'django.contrib.messages',
    'django.contrib.staticfiles',
    'movie',
]
...
```

Back in the Terminal, run the server:

For macOS, run with the following:

```
python3 manage.py runserver
```

For Windows, run with the following:

```
python manage.py runserver
```

The server should run without issues. We will learn more about apps throughout the course of this book.

Currently, you may notice a message in the Terminal when you run the server, as follows:

```
"You have 18 unapplied migration(s). Your project may not work
properly until you apply the migrations for app(s): admin,
auth, contenttypes, sessions.
Run 'python manage.py migrate' to apply them."
```

We will see how to address this problem later. But for now, remember that we can have one or more apps inside a project.

Summary

In this chapter, we discussed the Django project structure. We analyzed some of the most important project files and their functionalities. We saw how a web project can be composed of several applications, and we learned how to create a Django app. In the next chapter, we will see how to manage Django routes to provide the project with custom pages. And in upcoming chapters, we will see how the Django architecture model-view-template fits inside the Django project structure.

3
Managing Django URLs

Currently, we just have a default landing page provided by Django. How do we create our own custom pages and have different URLs to route to them? In this chapter, we will discuss how Django URLs work. We will learn how to define URLs and link them to respective Django views. In this chapter, we will be covering the following topic:

- Understanding and defining Django URLs

Technical requirements

In this chapter, we will be using Python 3.8+. Additionally, we will be using the **VS Code** editor in this book, which you can download from `https://code.visualstudio.com/`.

The code for this chapter is located at `https://github.com/PacktPublishing/Django-4-for-the-Impatient/tree/main/Chapter03/moviereviewsproject`.

Understanding and defining Django URLs

Remember that /moviereviews/urls.py is referenced each time someone types in a URL on our website – for example, localhost:8000/hello.

For now, we get an error page when we go to the preceding URL. So, how do we display a proper page for it? Each time a user types in a URL, the request passes through urls. py and sees whether the URL matches any defined paths so that the Django server can return an appropriate response.

urls.py currently has the following code:

```
from django.contrib import admin
from django.urls import path


urlpatterns = [
    path('admin/', admin.site.urls),
]
```

When a request passes through urls.py, it will try to match a path object in urlpatterns – for example, if a user enters http://localhost:8000/admin into the browser, the URL will match the admin/ path. The server will then respond with the Django admin site (as shown in *Figure 3.1*), which we will explore later:

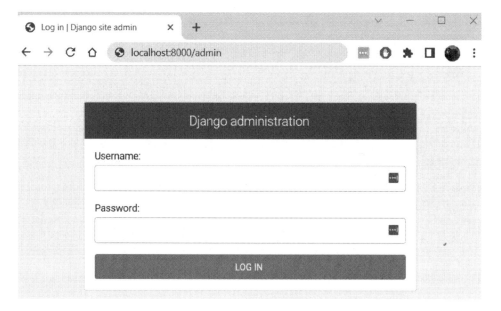

Figure 3.1 – The admin page

localhost:8000/hello, however, returns a 404 not found page because there aren't any matching paths.

Creating a custom path for a home page

To illustrate the creation of a custom path, let's create a path for a home page. Add the following code in **bold** into urls.py:

```
from django.contrib import admin
from django.urls import path
from movie import views as movieViews


urlpatterns = [
    path('admin/', admin.site.urls),
    path('', movieViews.home),
]
```

Let's explain the preceding code snippet:

```
urlpatterns = [
    path('admin/', admin.site.urls),
    path('', movieViews.home),
]
```

We added a new path object with the ' ' path – that is, it matches the localhost:8000/ URL for a home page. If there is such a match, we return movieViews.home, which is a function that returns the home page view:

```
from movie import views as movieViews
```

Where do we get movieViews.home from? We import it from /movie/views.py. Note that it is not /**moviereviews**/views.py. The views are stored in the individual apps themselves that is /movie/views.py. Because we have not defined the home function in /movie/views.py, let's proceed to do so:

/movie/views.py

In `views.py`, add the following in **bold**:

```
from django.shortcuts import render
from django.http import HttpResponse


def home(request):
    return HttpResponse('<h1>Welcome to Home Page</h1>')
```

We created a `home` function that returns an HTML markup in a `HTTPResponse`. We imported the built-in `HttpResponse` method to return a response object to the user. Save the file, and if you go back to `http://localhost:8000`, you should see the home page displayed (*Figure 3.2*):

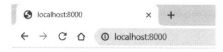

Figure 3.2 – Home page

Congratulations! We have added a new `localhost:8000/` home path that returns a home page. Now, let's try to create another path for an `About` page when a user navigates to `localhost:8000/about`. Commonly, About pages contain information about an application and its creators. We will just display a simple message.

Creating a custom path for an about page

In `/moviereviews/urls.py`, add the path in **bold**:

```
...
urlpatterns = [
    path('admin/', admin.site.urls),
    path('', movieViews.home),
    path('about/', movieViews.about),
]
```

So, if a URL matches the `about/` path, it will return the `about` function. Let's create the about function in `/movie/views.py`:

```
...
def home(request):
    return HttpResponse('<h1>Welcome to Home Page</h1>')


def about(request):
    return HttpResponse('<h1>Welcome to About Page</h1>')
```

Save the file, and when you navigate to `localhost:8000/about`, it will show the **About** page (*Figure 3.3*):

Welcome to About Page

Figure 3.3 – About page

> **Note**
> When we make changes to a file and save it, Django watches the file changes and reloads the server with the changes. Therefore, we don't have to manually restart the server each time there is a code change.

Summary

We now know how to create custom paths and linked them with respective view functions. Note that `urls.py` is located in the project's main folder, `moviereviews`. All requests to the site will go through `urls.py`. Then, specific paths defined in `urls.py` are linked to specific view functions, which are located in the individual app folders. For example, the `/about` path (defined in `urls.py` file) is linked to the `about` function (defined in the `/movie/views.py` file). This allows us to separate views according to the app they belong to.

So far, we are just returning simple HTML markups. What if we want to return full HTML pages? We can return them as what we are doing now. But it will be ideal if we can define the HTML page in a separate file of its own. Let's see how to do so in the next chapter.

4

Generating HTML Pages with Templates

Currently, we have a Django project with URLs connected to Django views. In those views, we defined functions that return HTML code. However, placing HTML code inside Django views is not a good strategy, and affects the project maintainability and evolution. We need to move away from HTML code to their own HTML files.

In this chapter, we will discuss how Django templates work. We will learn how to connect Django views to Django templates, separating HTML code from Django view code.

In this chapter, we will be covering the following topics:

- Understanding Django templates
- Passing data into templates
- Adding Bootstrap to our site
- Adding a search form
- Sending a form to another page

Technical requirements

In this chapter, we will be using Python 3.8+. Additionally, we will be using the **VS Code** editor in this book, which you can download from `https://code.visualstudio.com/`.

The code for this chapter is located at `https://github.com/PacktPublishing/Django-4-for-the-Impatient/tree/main/Chapter04/moviereviewsproject`.

Understanding Django templates

Every web framework needs a way to generate full HTML pages. In Django, we use `templates` to serve individual HTML files. In the `movie` folder, create a folder called `templates`. Each app should have its own templates folder (*Figure 4.1*).

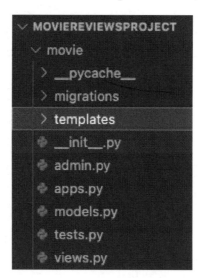

Figure 4.1 – Movie app directory structure

In the course of this book, you will see a pattern repeatedly in Django development – **templates**, **views**, and **URLs**. We have already worked with views and URLs in the previous chapter. The order between them doesn't matter, but all three are required and work closely together. Let's implement the template and refined view for the home page.

Template

In `/movie/templates/`, create a new file, `home.html`. This will be the full HTML page for the home page. For now, fill it in with the following:

```html
<!DOCTYPE html>
<html>
  <head>
    <title>Movies App</title>
  </head>

  <body>
    <h1>Welcome to Home Page</h1>
    <h2>This is the full home page</h2>
  </body>
</html>
```

As you can see, the template simply holds the HTML. It will display two messages with different HTML header tags.

View

Back in `/movie/views.py`, make the following change in **bold** to the home function:

```python
from django.shortcuts import render
from django.http import HttpResponse


def home(request):
    return render(request, 'home.html')
```

Note that we are now using `render` instead of `HttpResponse`, and in `render`, we specify `home.html` instead. So, we can continue to build up the HTML in `home.html`.

As you can see, the view contains the business logic or the "what." For now, we don't have much logic, but we shall explore views with more logic as we progress.

URLs

We earlier created the URL for our home and about pages in `/moviereviews/urls.py`:

```
...
urlpatterns = [
    path('admin/', admin.site.urls),
    path('', movieViews.home),
    path('about/', movieViews.about),
]
```

The URLs control the route and entry point into a page, such as the main `' '` path (the URL), which links to the `movieViews.home` (view) function that returns the `home.html` (template) code. You will see this pattern of templates, views, and URLs for almost every Django web page. As we repeat this multiple times throughout the book, you will begin to internalize it.

You can see the new home page if you go to `localhost:8000` (*Figure 4.2*):

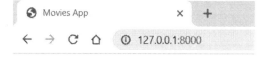

Welcome to Home Page

This is the full home page

Figure 4.2 – Home page

Now that we have understood how Django templates work, let's look at how we can pass data to the templates.

Passing data into templates

When rendering views, we can also pass in data. Add the following in bold to `/movie/views.py`:

```
...
def home(request):
    return render(request, 'home.html', {'name':'Greg
```

```
        Lim'})
    ...
```

We pass in a dictionary with a key-value pair (`{'name':'Greg Lim'}`) to `home.html`. And in `home.html`, we retrieve the dictionary values with the following in bold:

```
...

<body>
    <h1>Welcome to Home Page, {{ name }}</h1>
    <h2>This is the full home page</h2>
</body>

...
```

`{{ name }}` accesses the `'name'` key in the dictionary and thus retrieves the `'Greg Lim'` value. So, if you run the site now and go to the home page, you should see what is shown in *Figure 4.3*:

Welcome to Home Page, Greg Lim

This is the full home page

Figure 4.3 – A new home page

In the previous example, we used the variable syntax element from the **Django Template Language** (**DTL**). The DTL provides a set of elements and tags – for example, `{{ ... }}` and `{%. .. %}` – to help render HTML. You can see the full list of built-in elements and tags in the official docs: `https://docs.djangoproject.com/en/4.0/ref/templates/language/`.

We will introduce more DTL elements and tags and their usage as we progress.

Adding Bootstrap to our site

Before we go any further, let's add Bootstrap to our site. **Bootstrap** helps make our site look good without worrying about the necessary HTML/CSS to create a beautiful site. Bootstrap is the most popular framework for building responsive and mobile-friendly websites. Instead of writing our own CSS and JavaScript, we can choose which Bootstrap component we want to use – for example, a navigation bar, button, alert, list, and card – and simply copy and paste its markup into our template.

Let's look at the steps to do just that:

1. Go to `https://getbootstrap.com/` and go to **Get started** (*Figure 4.4*):

Figure 4.4 – The Bootstrap site

2. Copy the style sheet link (as shown in *Figure 4.5*) inside the `<head>` tag of the `home.html` template to load the Bootstrap CSS:

CSS

Copy-paste the stylesheet `<link>` into your `<head>` before all other stylesheets to load our CSS.

```
<link href="https://cdn.jsdelivr.net/npm/bootstrap@5.1.1/dist/css/bootstrap.min.css" re
```
Copy

Figure 4.5 – Bootstrap CSS CDN link

`home.html` will look something like this:

```
<!DOCTYPE html>
<html>
  <head>
```

```
<title>Movies App</title>
<link href=
  "https://cdn.jsdelivr.net/npm/bootstrap@5.1.1/
  dist/css/bootstrap.min.css" rel="stylesheet"
  crossorigin="anonymous">
</head>
...
```

3. You can immediately see the styling applied if you go to `localhost:8000` (as shown in *Figure 4.6*):

Figure 4.6 – Home page with Bootstrap

4. To improve the padding of the site, let's wrap the `home.html` HTML header tags in a `div` container:

```
...
<body>
  <div class="container">
    <h1>Welcome to Home Page, {{ name }}</h1>
    <h2>This is the full home page</h2>
  </div>
</body>
...
```

The result looks like this:

Figure 4.7 – Home page with the container

There are many other Bootstrap components we will use and add to our site. Next, we will use a form from Bootstrap!

Adding a search form

We will add a search form on our home page for users to search for movies. Let's get a Form component from *getbootstrap*. At `https://getbootstrap.com`, under **Docs**, go to **Forms | Overview** (as shown in *Figure 4.8*):

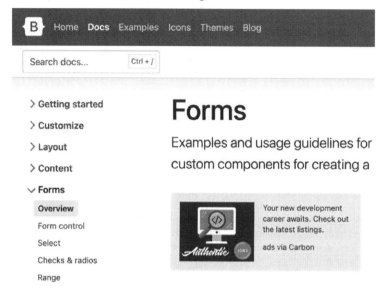

Figure 4.8 – Bootstrap forms

In the **Overview** section, you can copy the markup (as shown in *Figure 4.9*) and paste it inside the `home.html` template file. This is very useful because you will have a skeleton to design HTML forms with Bootstrap.

```
<form>
  <div class="mb-3">
    <label for="exampleInputEmail1" class="form-label">Email address</label>
    <input type="email" class="form-control" id="exampleInputEmail1" aria-describedby="ema
    <div id="emailHelp" class="form-text">We'll never share your email with anyone else.</
  </div>
  <div class="mb-3">
    <label for="exampleInputPassword1" class="form-label">Password</label>
    <input type="password" class="form-control" id="exampleInputPassword1">
  </div>
  <div class="mb-3 form-check">
    <input type="checkbox" class="form-check-input" id="exampleCheck1">
    <label class="form-check-label" for="exampleCheck1">Check me out</label>
  </div>
  <button type="submit" class="btn btn-primary">Submit</button>
</form>
```

Figure 4.9 – Bootstrap forms

Because we don't need much information from the previous form (such as `password` and `checkbox`), we refine the previous HTML code to only contain the **Search for Movie** field and a **Search** button. Add the following in bold to the `home.html` template file:

```
...
  <div class="container">
    <form action="">
      <div class="mb-3">
        <label class="form-label">Search for Movie:</label>
        <input type="text" name="searchMovie"
          class="form-control" />
      </div>
      <button type="submit" class="btn btn-primary">
        Search
      </button>
    </form>
  </div>
...
```

Now, you should have a simple search form (as shown in *Figure 4.10*):

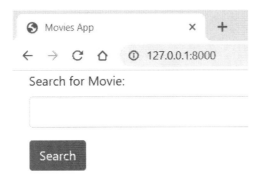

Figure 4.10 – Home page with form

For `input`, we specify `name="searchMovie"` to reference the input and retrieve its value. We have `action=""` in the form tag. The empty `""` string specifies that upon clicking on `submit`, we submit the form to the same page – that is, `home.html`. If we want to submit the form to another page – for example, the about page – we will have `<form action="{% url 'about' %}">`. We will illustrate this in the next section. For now, we submit to the same page.

movie/views.py

Now, how do we retrieve the values submitted? Because the form submits to `""`, which `urls.py` routes to `def home` in `movie/views.py`, we can retrieve the values from the request object in `def home` (add the following code in bold):

```
...
def home(request):
    searchTerm = request.GET.get('searchMovie')
    return render(request, 'home.html',
      {'searchTerm':searchTerm})
...
```

By default, a form submission sends a `GET` request if the type of request is not specified. Thus, we access the request with `request.GET` and specify the name of the input field, `searchMovie` – that is, `request.GET.get('searchMovie')` – to get the input value. We assign the input value to `searchTerm`.

movie/templates/home.html

We then pass `searchTerm` into `home.html` in the render function with `{'searchTerm':searchTerm}`. Add the following code in bold to `home.html`:

```
...
    <form action="">
      ...
    </form>
    Searching for {{ searchTerm }}
  </div>
...
```

When we run our app, enter a value in the search form and hit **Search**:

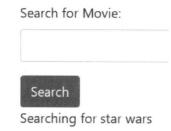

Figure 4.11 – Home page with the form completed

The page reloads and the search term appears after the form (as shown in *Figure 4.11*).

Sending a form to another page

Currently, we submit a form to the same page. Suppose we want to submit a form to another page – how do we do that? Let's illustrate by having a **Join our mailing list** form below the search form. Add the following markup to `home.html`:

```
...
  <div class="container">
    <form action="">
      ...
    </form>
    Searching for {{ searchTerm }}
    <br />
    <br />
    <h2>Join our mailing list:</h2>
    <form action="{% url 'signup' %}">
      <div class="mb-3">
        <label for="email" class="form-label">
          Enter your email:
        </label>
        <input type="email" class="form-control"
          name="email" />
      </div>
      <button type="submit" class="btn btn-primary">
        Sign Up
      </button>
    </form>
  </div>
...
```

The signup form is similar to the search form. We have an `email` input and a `Sign Up` button. What is different is in the `<form>` tag, `<form action="{% url 'signup' %}">`.

The `url` template tag `{% url 'signup' %}` takes a URL pattern name – for example `'signup'` – and returns a URL link.

Let's now add the `'signup'` route to `urlpatterns` in `/moviereviews/urls.py`:

```
...
urlpatterns = [
    path('admin/', admin.site.urls),
    path('', movieViews.home),
    path('about/', movieViews.about),
    path('signup/', movieViews.signup, name='signup'),
]
```

This time, we provide an optional URL name, `'signup'`, to the `path` object. In doing so, we can then refer to this URL, name=`'signup'`, from the URL template tag, `{% url 'signup' %}`. The URL tag uses these names to create links for us automatically. While it's optional to add a named URL, it's a best practice we should adopt, as it helps keep things organized as the number of URLs grows.

/movie/views.py

Next, in `movie/views.py`, add the `signup` function (similar to `home`):

```
...


def signup(request):
    email = request.GET.get('email')
    return render(request, 'signup.html', {'email':email})
```

We retrieve the email from the GET request (`request.GET.get('email')`) and send it to `signup.html` by passing in a key-value pair dictionary, `{'email':email}`.

In `movie/templates/`, create a new file, `signup.html`, with the following markup:

```
<!DOCTYPE html>
<html>
  <head>
    <title>Movies App</title>
    <link href="https://cdn.jsdelivr.net/npm/
      bootstrap@5.1.1/dist/css/bootstrap.min.css"
      rel="stylesheet" crossorigin="anonymous">
  </head>
```

```
  <body>
    <div class="container">
      <h2>Added {{ email }} to mailing list</h2>
    </div>
  </body>
</html>
```

When you run your site, add a valid email to the signup form and click **Sign Up** (as shown in *Figure 4.12*):

Join our mailing list:

Enter your email:

greg@greglim.com

Sign Up

Figure 4.12 – Home page with the signup form filled in

You will be brought to the signup page (`signup.html`) with a response message (as shown in *Figure 4.13*):

Added greg@greglim.com to mailing list

Figure 4.13 – Signup page

Note the URL in `signup.html`. It will be something like `http://localhost:8000/signup/?email=greg%40greglim.com`.

This is the URL that is sent in the GET request. You can see the parameters being passed in via the URL. But what if you have a login form that passes in a username and password? You will want this hidden in the URL. We will later see how to send a POST request from a form that hides the values passed in.

Creating a back link

Suppose we want to create a link from `signup.html` back to `home.html`. We can do so using the `<a>` tag. In `signup.html`, add the line in bold:

```
...
    <div class="container">
       <h2>Added {{ email }} to mailing list</h2>
       <a href="{% url 'home' %}">Home</a>
    </div>
...
```

And in `/moviereviews/urls.py`, add the following in bold:

```
...
urlpatterns = [
    path('admin/', admin.site.urls),
    path('', movieViews.home, name='home'),
    path('about/', movieViews.about, name='about'),
    path('signup/', movieViews.signup, name='signup'),
]
```

We added `name='home'` to configure a URL route for our home page, `{% url 'home' %}`. We also added `name='about'` to configure a URL route for our about page.

If you go to `signup.html`, you will see the following:

Figure 4.14 – Signup page with a back link

There will be a link to navigate back to home (as shown in *Figure 4.14*).

Summary

By now, you should have a better grasp of what happens when a user types a URL into the browser, sends a request to our site, goes through `urls.py`, connects to a Django view, and our Django server uses a template to respond with HTML. We hope this serves as a solid foundation to move on to the next part of our project, where we will go through more advanced topics such as models to make our site database-driven.

5
Working
with Models

Storing data in a database is a common practice in most web applications. In a Django project, it involves working with Django models. We will create a database model (for example, blog posts and movies) and Django will turn this model into a database table for us. We will also explore a powerful built-in admin interface that provides a visual way of managing all aspects of a Django project, such as managing users and making changes to model data.

In this chapter, we will be covering the following topics:

- Creating our first model
- Managing migrations
- Accessing the Django admin interface
- Configuring for images
- Serving stored images
- Adding a movie model to admin

Technical requirements

In this chapter, we will be using Python 3.8+. Additionally, we will be using the **VS Code** editor in this book, which you can download from `https://code.visualstudio.com/`.

The code for this chapter is located at `https://github.com/PacktPublishing/Django-4-for-the-Impatient/tree/main/Chapter05/moviereviewsproject`.

Creating our first model

Working with databases in Django involves working with models. A **model** contains the fields and behaviors of the data we want to store. Commonly, each model maps a database table. We can create models such as blog posts, movies, and users, and Django turns these models into a database table for us.

Here are the Django model basics:

- Each model is a class that extends `django.db.models.Model`.

- Each model attribute represents a database column.

- With all of this, Django provides us with a set of useful methods to **create, update, read, and delete** (**CRUD**) model information from a database.

/movie/models.py

In `/movie`, we have the `models.py` file, where we create our models for the movie app. Open that file and fill it in with the following:

```python
from django.db import models


class Movie(models.Model):
    title = models.CharField(max_length=100)
    description = models.CharField(max_length=250)
    image = models.ImageField(upload_to='movie/images/')
    url = models.URLField(blank=True)
```

Let's look at what happens in this code:

```python
from django.db import models
```

We import the models module from django.db. This module helps to define and map the characteristics of the model into the database. In our case, we created a Movie model to store the title, description, image, and url of a movie.

```
class Movie(models.Model):
```

class Movie inherits from the Model class. The Model class allows us to interact with the database, create a table, and retrieve and make changes to data in the database:

```
title = models.CharField(max_length=100)
description = models.CharField(max_length=250)
image = models.ImageField(upload_to='movie/images/')
url = models.URLField(blank=True)
```

We then have the properties of the model. Note that the properties have types such as CharField, ImageField, and URLField. Django provides many other model fields to support common types such as dates, integers, and emails. To have a complete documentation of the kinds of types and how to use them, refer to the Model field reference in the Django documentation (https://docs.djangoproject.com/en/4.0/ref/models/fields/). For example, CharField is a string field for small-to-large-sized strings, and the max_length argument is required (as shown in *Figure 5.1*):

CharField

class CharField(*max_length=None, **options*)

A string field, for small- to large-sized strings.

For large amounts of text, use **TextField**.

The default form widget for this field is a **TextInput**.

CharField has two extra arguments:

CharField.max_length

Required. The maximum length (in characters) of the field. using **MaxLengthValidator**.

Figure 5.1 – CharField documentation

Let's understand the preceding code snippet.

We assign CharField to both title and description. image is of ImageField, and we specify the upload_to option to specify a subdirectory of MEDIA_ROOT (found in settings.py) to use for uploaded images. url is of URLField, a CharField for a URL. Because not all movies have URLs, we specify blank=True to indicate that this field is optional.

We will use this model to create a movie table in our database.

Installing pillow

Because we are using images, we need to install Pillow (https://pypi.org/project/Pillow/), which adds image processing capabilities to our Python interpreter.

In the Terminal, stop the server and run the following.

For macOS, run this:

```
pip3 install pillow
```

For Windows, run this:

```
pip install pillow
```

Managing migrations

Migrations allow us to generate a database schema based on model code. Once we make changes to our models (such as adding a field and renaming a field), new migrations should be created. In the end, migrations allow us to have a trace of the evolution of our database schema (as a version control system).

Currently, note a message in the Terminal when you run the server:

```
"You have 18 unapplied migration(s). Your project may not work
properly until you apply the migrations for app(s): admin,
auth, contenttypes, sessions.
Run 'python manage.py migrate' to apply them."
```

As per the message instructions, run the following.

For macOS, run this:

```
python3 manage.py migrate
```

For Windows, run this:

```
python manage.py migrate
```

The `migrate` command creates an initial database based on Django's default settings. Note that there is a `db.sqlite3` file in the project root folder. The file represents our SQLite database. It is created the first time we run either `migrate` or `runserver`. `runserver` configures the database using Django's default settings. In the previous case, the `migrate` command applied 18 default migrations (as shown in *Figure 5.2*). Those migrations were defined by some default Django apps – `admin`, `auth`, `contenttypes`, and `sessions`. These apps are loaded in the `INSTALLED_APPS` variable in the `moviereviews/settings.py` file. So, the `migrate` command runs the migrations of all the installed apps. Note that `INSTALLED_APPS` also loads the `movie` app. However, no migrations were applied for the `movie` app. This is because we have not generated the migrations for the `movie` app:

```
[MacBook-Air:moviereviewsproject user$ python3 manage.py migrate
Operations to perform:
  Apply all migrations: admin, auth, contenttypes, sessions
Running migrations:
  Applying contenttypes.0001_initial... OK
  Applying auth.0001_initial... OK
  Applying admin.0001_initial... OK
  Applying admin.0002_logentry_remove_auto_add... OK
  Applying admin.0003_logentry_add_action_flag_choices... OK
  Applying contenttypes.0002_remove_content_type_name... OK
  Applying auth.0002_alter_permission_name_max_length... OK
  Applying auth.0003_alter_user_email_max_length... OK
  Applying auth.0004_alter_user_username_opts... OK
  Applying auth.0005_alter_user_last_login_null... OK
  Applying auth.0006_require_contenttypes_0002... OK
  Applying auth.0007_alter_validators_add_error_messages... OK
  Applying auth.0008_alter_user_username_max_length... OK
  Applying auth.0009_alter_user_last_name_max_length... OK
  Applying auth.0010_alter_group_name_max_length... OK
  Applying auth.0011_update_proxy_permissions... OK
  Applying auth.0012_alter_user_first_name_max_length... OK
  Applying sessions.0001_initial... OK_
```

Figure 5.2 – Applying default Django migrations

Let's create the migrations for the `movie` app. We will run the `makemigrations` command in the Terminal.

For macOS, run this:

```
python3 manage.py makemigrations
```

For Windows, run this:

```
python manage.py makemigrations
```

This generates the SQL commands for the defined models in all preinstalled apps in our `INSTALLED_APPS` setting. The SQL commands are not yet executed but are just a record of all changes to our models. The migrations are stored in an auto-generated folder, `migrations` (as shown in *Figure 5.3*):

Figure 5.3 – Generated migrations for the movie app

Then, we need to build the actual database with `migrate` (`python3 manage. py migrate`), which executes the SQL commands in the migrations file. Currently, it uses the default SQLite database engine, but you can integrate your own DB system by modifying the `moviereviews/settings.py` file. Now, execute the following in the Terminal.

For macOS, run this:

```
python3 manage.py migrate
```

For Windows, run this:

```
python manage.py migrate
```

As you can see in *Figure 5.4*, we applied the movie migrations:

```
Operations to perform:
  Apply all migrations: admin, auth, contenttypes, movie, sessions
Running migrations:
  Applying movie.0001_initial... OK
```

Figure 5.4 – Applying the movie migrations

In summary, each time you make changes to a model file, you have to run the following.

For macOS, run this:

```
python3 manage.py makemigrations
python3 manage.py migrate
```

For Windows, run this:

```
python manage.py makemigrations
python manage.py migrate
```

But how do we access our database and view what's inside? For that, we use a powerful tool in Django called the admin interface, which there will be more on in the next section.

Accessing the Django admin interface

To access our database, we have to go into the Django admin interface. Remember that there is an admin path in /moviereviews/urls.py?

```
...
urlpatterns = [
    path('admin/', admin.site.urls),
    path('', movieViews.home),
    path('about/', movieViews.about),
    path('signup/', movieViews.signup, name='signup'),
]
```

If you go to `localhost:8000/admin`, it brings you to the admin site (as shown in *Figure 5.5*):

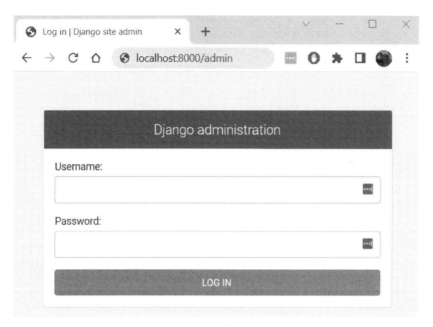

Figure 5.5 – Admin page

Django has a powerful built-in admin interface that provides a visual way of managing all aspects of a Django project – for example, managing users and making changes to model data.

With what username and password do we log in to Admin? We will have to first create a superuser in the Terminal.

In the Terminal, run the following.

For macOS, run this:

```
python3 manage.py createsuperuser
```

For Windows, run this:

```
python manage.py createsuperuser
```

You will then be asked to specify a username, email, and password. Note that anyone can access the admin path on your site, so make sure that your password is something secure.

If you wish to change your password later, you can run the following commands.

For macOS, run this:

```
python3 manage.py changepassword <username>
```

For Windows, run this:

```
python manage.py changepassword <username>
```

Then, start the server again, and log into admin with the username you have just created (as shown in *Figure 5.6*):

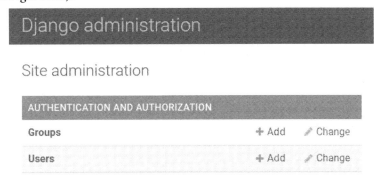

Figure 5.6 – Site administration page

Under **Users**, you will see the user you have just created (as shown in *Figure 5.7*):

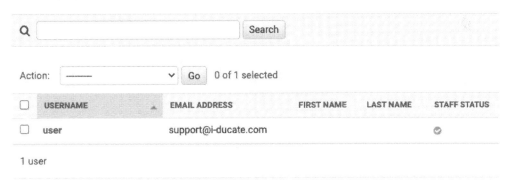

Figure 5.7 – Users admin page

You can add additional user accounts here for your team.

Currently, our movie model doesn't show up in admin. We need to explicitly tell Django what to display in it. Before adding our movie model in admin, let's first configure our images.

Configuring for images

We have to configure where to store our images when we add them. First, go to `moviereviews/settings.py` and add the following at the bottom of the file:

```
...
MEDIA_ROOT = os.path.join(BASE_DIR,'media')
MEDIA_URL = '/media/'
```

At the top of the file, add the following:

```
import os
```

Here, `MEDIA_ROOT` is the absolute filesystem path to the directory that will hold user-uploaded files, and we join `BASE_DIR` with `'media'`. Also, `MEDIA_URL` is the URL that handles the media served from `MEDIA_ROOT` (refer to `https://docs.djangoproject.com/en/4.0/ref/settings/` to find out more about the setting properties).

When we add a movie in admin (explained in the *Adding a movie model to admin* section later in this chapter), you will see the image stored inside the `/moviereviews/media/` folder.

Serving the stored images

Next, to enable the server to serve the stored images, we have to add to `/moviereviews/urls.py` the following:

```
...
from django.conf.urls.static import static
from django.conf import settings

urlpatterns = [

    ...
]

urlpatterns += static(settings.MEDIA_URL,
   document_root=settings.MEDIA_ROOT)
```

With this, you can serve the static media from Django. Having configured the images, let's add our movie model to the admin panel.

Adding a movie model to admin

To add the movie model to admin, go back to /movie/admin.py, and register our model with the following:

```python
from django.contrib import admin
from .models import Movie


admin.site.register(Movie)
```

When you save your file, go back to admin. The movie model will now show up (as shown in *Figure 5.8*):

Figure 5.8 – Admin page

Try adding a `movie` object by clicking on **+Add**. You will be brought to the **Add movie** form (as shown in *Figure 5.9*):

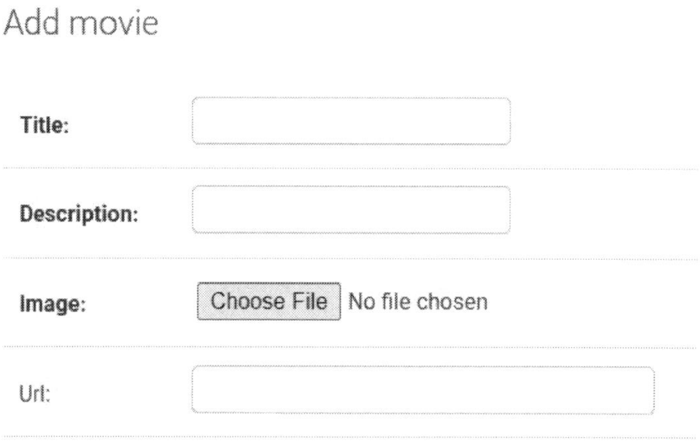

Add movie

Title:

Description:

Image: Choose File   No file chosen

Url:

Figure 5.9 – Add movie page

Note that **Url** is not in bold, as we marked it as optional back in `models.py`, `url = models.URLField(blank=True)`. The other required fields are in bold.

Try adding a movie and hit **Save**. Your movie object will be saved to the database and reflected in the admin page (as shown in *Figure 5.10*):

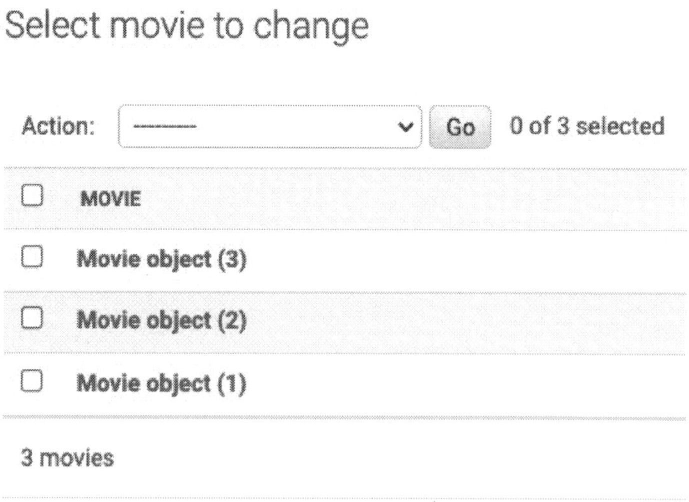

Select movie to change

Action: [-------- ▾] [Go]   0 of 3 selected

☐ **MOVIE**

☐ **Movie object (3)**

☐ **Movie object (2)**

☐ **Movie object (1)**

3 movies

Figure 5.10 – Movies admin page

You can also see the movie image in `/moviereviews/media/movie/images/<image file>.jpg`.

Summary

Models are essential to work with databases in Django. We learned the fundamentals of Django models and created a movie model. We also learned to use the Django admin interface and how to create movies. Now, let's see how we can display these movies on our site in the next chapter.

6
Displaying Objects from Admin

Previously, we learned how to store data in a database. In this chapter, we will collect and display database information. We will display movie information and use some Bootstrap cards to improve the look and feel of our app. Then, we will create a news app with its respective model, view, templates, and URLs. Finally, we will display the news information.

In this chapter, we will be covering the following topics:

- Listing movies
- Using the card component
- Implementing a search
- Adding a news app
- Listing news

Technical requirements

In this chapter, we will be using Python 3.8+. Additionally, we will be using the **VS Code** editor in this book, which you can download from `https://code.visualstudio.com/`.

The code for this chapter is located at `https://github.com/PacktPublishing/Django-4-for-the-Impatient/tree/main/Chapter06/moviereviewsproject`.

Listing movies

Let's improve our app. We will display the movie objects stored in the admin database. In `movie/views.py`, add the following in bold:

```
...
from .models import Movie

def home(request):
    searchTerm = request.GET.get('searchMovie')
    movies = Movie.objects.all()
    return render(request, 'home.html',
        {'searchTerm':searchTerm, 'movies': movies})
...
```

Let's look at what's happening in the code. We first import the `Movie` model:

```
from .models import Movie
```

Then, the previous code grabs all the movie objects from the database (using the `all` method) and assigns them to `movies`:

```
movies = Movie.objects.all()
```

We then pass `movies` in the dictionary to `home.html`.

Django makes it really straightforward to access objects in the database. If we have to write code to connect to the database, write SQL statements for retrieval, and convert the results to Python objects, it will involve a lot more code! But Django provides lots of database functionality to handle these for us. You can find a full list of the available methods here: `https://docs.djangoproject.com/en/4.0/topics/db/queries/`.

/movie/templates/home.html

In `home.html`, we display the objects by adding the following code in bold:

```
...
<body>
  <div class="container">
    <form action="">
      ...
    </form>
    <p>Searching for: {{ searchTerm }}</p>
    {% for movie in movies %}
      <h2>{{ movie.title }}</h2>
      <h3>{{ movie.description }}</h3>
      <img src="{{ movie.image.url }}">
      {% if movie.url %}
        <a href="{{ movie.url }}">Movie Link</a>
      {% endif %}
    {% endfor %}
    <br />
    <br />
    <h2>Join our mailing list:</h2>
    ...
```

Let's understand what's happening here:

```
{% for movie in movies %}
    ...
{% endfor %}
```

Using a `for` loop in the Django templating language, we loop through `movies`, with `movie` acting as a temporary variable to hold the element for the current iteration. Note that we enclose code in {% ... %} template tags. We use {{ ... }} to render variables such as a movie's title, description, and image URL, as shown in the following example:

```
<h2>{{ movie.title }}</h2>
<h3>{{ movie.description }}</h3>
<img src="{{ movie.image.url }}">
```

Because a movie URL is optional, which means it can be null, we check whether it has a value with {% if movie.url %} and, if so, render a `<a>` href to the movie URL:

```
{% if movie.url %}
  <a href="{{ movie.url }}">Movie Link</a>
{% endif %}
```

We presented a practical use of both the `for` and `if` template tags. You can find a more complete list of template tags here: `https://docs.djangoproject.com/en/4.0/ref/templates/language/#tags`.

When you run your site and go to the home page, you will see the movies you added (in admin) on the page (as shown in *Figure 6.1*):

Searching for: None

Gladiator

Gladiator is a 2000 epic historical drama film directed by Ridley Scott and written by David Franzoni, John Logan, and William Nicholson.

Movie Link

Figure 6.1 – Home page listing movies

If you add another movie in admin, it will be listed on the website when you reload it.

Let's further improve the look of our site by using the card component from Bootstrap to display each movie (`https://getbootstrap.com/docs/5.1/components/card/`).

Using the card component

Each movie will be displayed in a card component. In `movie/templates/home.html`, replace the `for` loop markup and make the following changes in bold:

```
...
<body>
  <div class="container">
    <form action="">
      ...
    </form>
    <p>Searching for: {{ searchTerm }}</p>
    <div class="row row-cols-1 row-cols-md-3 g-4">
      {% for movie in movies %}
      <div v-for="movie in movies" class="col">
        <div class="card">
          <img class="card-img-top" src="{{
            movie.image.url }}" />
          <div class="card-body">
            <h5 class="card-title fw-bold">{{ movie.title
              }}</h5>
            <p class="card-text">{{ movie.description
              }}</p>
            {% if movie.url %}
            <a href="{{ movie.url }}"
              class="btn btn-primary">
              Movie Link
            </a>
            {% endif %}
          </div>
        </div>
      </div>
    </div>
```

```
    {% endfor %}
</div>
<br />
<br />
<h2>Join our mailing list:</h2>
...
```

The home page should look something like *Figure 6.2*:

Searching for: None

Gladiator

Gladiator is a 2000 epic historical drama film directed by Ridley Scott and written by David Franzoni, John Logan, and William Nicholson.

Movie Link

Fast & Furious 9

F9 (also known as F9: The Fast Saga and internationally as Fast & Furious 9) is a 2021 action film directed by Justin Lin from a screenplay by Daniel Casey and Lin.

Harry Potter and the Half-Blood Prince

Harry Potter and the Half-Blood Prince is a 2009 fantasy film directed by David Yates and distributed by Warner Bros. It is based on J. K. Rowling's 2005 novel of the same name.

Figure 6.2 – Home page listing movies with the card component

We are currently listing all movies in our database. In the next section, let's display only the movies that fit the user-entered search term.

Implementing a search

Implement `def home` in `/movie/views.py` with the following (remove the old `def home` function and paste the next one):

```
def home(request):
    searchTerm = request.GET.get('searchMovie')
    if searchTerm:
        movies =
            Movie.objects.filter(title__icontains=searchTerm)
    else:
        movies = Movie.objects.all()
    return render(request, 'home.html',
      {'searchTerm':searchTerm, 'movies': movies})
```

Let's see what's happening in the code. We retrieve the search term entered (if any) from the `searchMovie` input:

```
    searchTerm = request.GET.get('searchMovie')
```

If a search term is entered, we call the model's `filter` method to return the movie objects with a case-insensitive match to the search term:

```
    if searchTerm:
        movies =
            Movie.objects.filter(title__icontains=searchTerm)
```

If there is no search term entered, we simply return all movies:

```
    else:
        movies = Movie.objects.all()
```

Now, when you run your app and enter a search term, the site displays only the movies that fit the search term.

Up to this point, we have covered a lot of material. Let's now crystallize and recap the concepts learned by adding a news app to our site. We currently have one app, `movie`, in our project. Let's add a `news` app.

Adding a news app

Do you remember how to add an app, add a model, and then display objects from the admin database? Try it on your own as a challenge.

Have you tried it? Let's now go through it together. To add a news app, run the following in the Terminal:

- macOS:

```
python3 manage.py startapp news
```

- Windows:

```
python manage.py startapp news
```

A news folder will be added to the project.

/moviereviews/settings.py

Each time we add an app, we have to tell Django about it by adding it to moviereviews/settings.py:

```
...
INSTALLED_APPS = [
    'django.contrib.admin',
    'django.contrib.auth',
    'django.contrib.contenttypes',
    'django.contrib.sessions',
    'django.contrib.messages',
    'django.contrib.staticfiles',
    'movie',
    'news',
]
...
```

Next, we have to add the path to news in /moviereviews/urls.py. Note that in urls.py, we have quite a few existing paths for the movie app:

```
...
urlpatterns = [
    path('admin/', admin.site.urls),
```

```
    path('', movieViews.home, name='home'),
    path('about/', movieViews.about, name='about'),
    path('signup/', movieViews.signup, name='signup'),
]
...
```

If we were to add the paths for news, the number of paths would increase, and it would soon be difficult to distinguish which paths are for which app (especially when the project grows). To better segregate the paths into their own apps, each app can have its own urls.py.

First, in /moviereviews/urls.py, add the following in bold:

```
...
from django.contrib import admin
from django.urls import path, include
...

urlpatterns = [
    path('admin/', admin.site.urls),
    path('', movieViews.home, name='home'),
    path('about/', movieViews.about, name='about'),
    path('signup/', movieViews.signup, name='signup'),
    path('news/', include('news.urls')),
]
...
```

path('news/', include('news.url')) will forward any requests with 'news/' to the news app's urls.py.

In /news, create a new file, urls.py, with the following:

```
from django.urls import path
from . import views

urlpatterns = [
    path('', views.news, name='news'),
]
```

The preceding path forwards a request – for example, `localhost:8000/news` – to the news view.

Next, in `/news/views.py`, add the `def news` function:

```
from django.shortcuts import render


def news(request):
    return render(request, 'news.html')
```

In `/news`, we now need to create the `templates` folder and, in it, a new file, `news.html`. We will later populate this file to display news articles from the admin database.

News model

Let's first create the `News` model:

1. In `/news/models.py`, create the model with the following:

    ```
    from django.db import models


    class News(models.Model):
        headline = models.CharField(max_length=200)
        body = models.TextField()
        date = models.DateField()
    ```

    Because we have added a new model, we need to make migrations:

2. For macOS, make migrations with the following:

    ```
    python3 manage.py makemigrations
    python3 manage.py migrat
    ```

    For Windows, make migrations with the following:

    ```
    python manage.py makemigrations
    python manage.py migr3te
    ```

3. Next, register the news model by going to `/news/admin.py` and adding the following in bold:

```
from django.contrib import admin
from .models import News


admin.site.register(News)
```

When you run the server and go to admin now, it should reflect the news model (as shown in *Figure 6.3*):

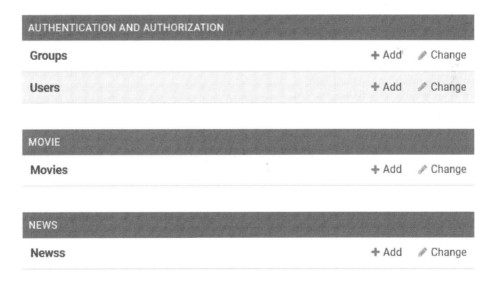

Figure 6.3 – Admin page with news

Listing news

Let's go ahead and display the news articles in `news.html`:

1. In `/news/views.py`, add the following in bold:

```python
from django.shortcuts import render
from .models import News


def news(request):
    newss = News.objects.all()
    return render(request, 'news.html',
      {'newss':newss})
```

We retrieve the news objects from the database and then pass them to `news.html`.

2. In `/news/templates/news.html`, display the news objects with the following code:

```html
<!DOCTYPE html>
<html>
  <head>
    <title>Movies App</title>
    <link href="https://cdn.jsdelivr.net/npm/
      bootstrap@5.1.1/dist/css/bootstrap.min.css"
      rel="stylesheet" crossorigin="anonymous">
  </head>
  <body>
    <div class="container">
      {% for news in newss %}
      <h2>{{ news.headline }}</h2>
      <h5>{{ news.date }}</h5>
      <p>{{ news.body }}</p>
      {% endfor %}
    </div>
  </body>
</html>
```

3. Now, try adding some news objects in admin. When you visit `http://localhost:8000/news/`, you should see them displayed (as shown in *Figure 6.4*):

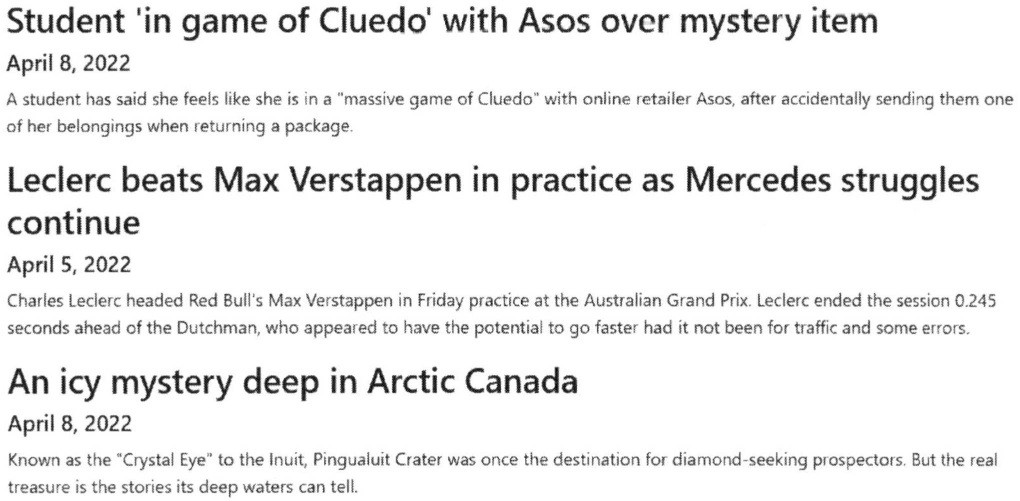

Student 'in game of Cluedo' with Asos over mystery item

April 8, 2022

A student has said she feels like she is in a "massive game of Cluedo" with online retailer Asos, after accidentally sending them one of her belongings when returning a package.

Leclerc beats Max Verstappen in practice as Mercedes struggles continue

April 5, 2022

Charles Leclerc headed Red Bull's Max Verstappen in Friday practice at the Australian Grand Prix. Leclerc ended the session 0.245 seconds ahead of the Dutchman, who appeared to have the potential to go faster had it not been for traffic and some errors.

An icy mystery deep in Arctic Canada

April 8, 2022

Known as the "Crystal Eye" to the Inuit, Pingualuit Crater was once the destination for diamond-seeking prospectors. But the real treasure is the stories its deep waters can tell.

Figure 6.4 – News page

When displaying news, we should be displaying the most recent news first. To do this, we can order the news objects in /news/views.py by specifying `order_by`:

```
from django.shortcuts import render
from .models import News


def news(request):
    newss = News.objects.all().order_by('-date')
    return render(request, 'news.html', {'newss':newss})
```

The most recent news will now be displayed first (as shown in *Figure 6.5*):

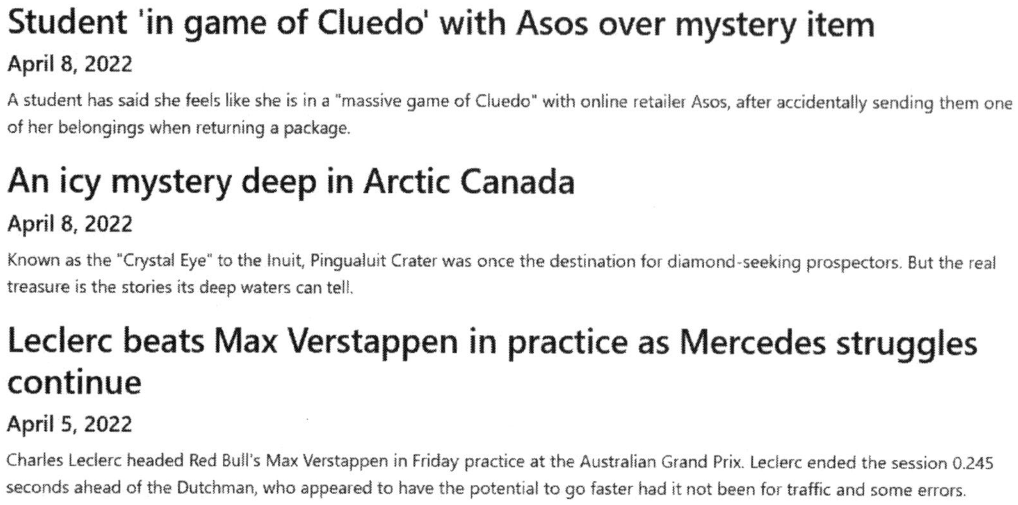

Student 'in game of Cluedo' with Asos over mystery item

April 8, 2022

A student has said she feels like she is in a "massive game of Cluedo" with online retailer Asos, after accidentally sending them one of her belongings when returning a package.

An icy mystery deep in Arctic Canada

April 8, 2022

Known as the "Crystal Eye" to the Inuit, Pingualuit Crater was once the destination for diamond-seeking prospectors. But the real treasure is the stories its deep waters can tell.

Leclerc beats Max Verstappen in practice as Mercedes struggles continue

April 5, 2022

Charles Leclerc headed Red Bull's Max Verstappen in Friday practice at the Australian Grand Prix. Leclerc ended the session 0.245 seconds ahead of the Dutchman, who appeared to have the potential to go faster had it not been for traffic and some errors.

Figure 6.5 – News page with news ordered by date

We should also improve the look of the news site with the Bootstrap Horizontal Card component (https://getbootstrap.com/docs/5.1/components/card/#horizontal). In /news/templates/news.html, replace the for loop markup and make the following changes in bold:

```
...
<body>
  <div class="container">
    {% for news in newss %}
    <div class="card mb-3">
      <div class="row g-0">
        <div>
          <div class="card-body">
            <h5 class="card-title">{{ news.headline
              }}</h5>
            <p class="card-text">{{ news.body }}</p>
            <p class="card-text"><small
              class="text-muted">
              {{ news.date }}
            </small></p>
          </div>
```

```
            </div>
         </div>
      </div>
      {% endfor %}
   </div>
 </body>
</html>
```

You should get something like *Figure 6.6*:

Student 'in game of Cluedo' with Asos over mystery item

A student has said she feels like she is in a "massive game of Cluedo" with online retailer Asos, after accidentally sending them one of her belongings when returning a package.

April 8, 2022

An icy mystery deep in Arctic Canada

Known as the "Crystal Eye" to the Inuit, Pingualuit Crater was once the destination for diamond-seeking prospectors. But the real treasure is the stories its deep waters can tell.

April 8, 2022

Leclerc beats Max Verstappen in practice as Mercedes struggles continue

Charles Leclerc headed Red Bull's Max Verstappen in Friday practice at the Australian Grand Prix. Leclerc ended the session 0.245 seconds ahead of the Dutchman, who appeared to have the potential to go faster had it not been for traffic and some errors.

April 5, 2022

Figure 6.6 – News page with the horizontal card component

Summary

We hope that this chapter crystalizes your understanding of adding an app to the project, adding a model, and displaying model objects from the database in the template. In the next chapter, we go deeper into understanding how the database works.

7

Understanding the Database

We have used Django models to persist data. In this chapter, we will inspect how databases work in Django. We will also improve the admin page readability and show how to switch between database engines.

In this chapter, we will be covering the following topics:

- Understanding the database viewer
- Displaying object information in admin
- Switching to a MySQL database

Technical requirements

In this chapter, we will be using Python 3.8+. Additionally, we will be using the **VS Code** editor in this book, which you can download from `https://code.visualstudio.com/`.

The code for this chapter is located at `https://github.com/PacktPublishing/Django-4-for-the-Impatient/tree/main/Chapter07/moviereviewsproject`.

Understanding the database viewer

Let's take some time to understand how the database works. The objects are stored in the db.sqlite3 file. If you click on it, it is not very readable. But you can view such SQlite files with a SQLite viewer; just google SQLite Viewer for a list of them. One example is https://inloop.github.io/sqlite-viewer/.

Drag and drop your db.sqlite3 file into the previous link (over the SQLite viewer), and you can see the different tables in the database (as shown in *Figure 7.1*):

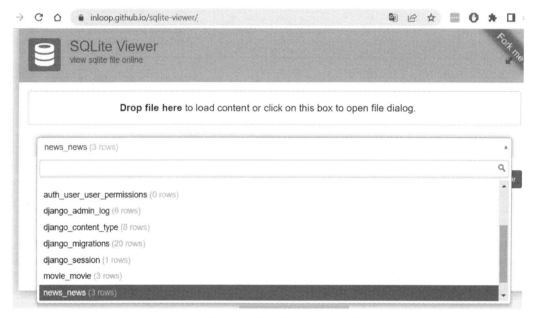

Figure 7.1 – Opening db.sqlite3 in SQLite Viewer

You can see the tables of the models we have created – that is, movie and news. There are other tables, such as django_session, because of the different apps that are installed for functions such as sessions and authentications.

Select a table – for example, news_news, and you can see its rows (*Figure 7.2*).

> **Note**
>
> The table name is derived from <appname>_<modelname>. We can have multiple models in an app – for example, movie_movie, movie_review.

Figure 7.2 – Opening db.sqlite3 in SQLite Viewer

Note that each row has a Django-generated unique ID as a primary key. Django automatically adds a primary key to each table.

So, hopefully this lets you appreciate what goes on behind the scenes in a Django database. Currently, we are using a SQL-based database. What if we want to switch to some other database – for example, NoSQL, PostgreSQL, Oracle, or MySQL? Django provides built-in support for several types of database backends.

To switch to another database engine, you can go to /moviereviews/settings.py and make changes to the lines in bold:

```
...
DATABASES = {
    'default': {
        'ENGINE': 'django.db.backends.sqlite3',
        'NAME': BASE_DIR / 'db.sqlite3',
    }
}
...
```

You can still create your models as per normal, and the changes are handled by Django behind the scenes.

In the book, we are using SQLite because it is the simplest. Django uses SQLite by default, and it's a great choice for small projects. It runs off a single file and doesn't require complex installation. In contrast, the other options involve some complexity to configure them properly. We will see at the end of this chapter how to configure a more robust database.

Displaying object information in admin

Currently, when we look at our model objects in admin, it is hard to identify individual objects (as shown in *Figure 7.3*) – for example, **News object (1)** and **News object (2)**:

Select news to change

| Action: | ———— ⌄ | Go | 0 of 3 selected |

☐ **NEWS**

☐ News object (3)

☐ News object (2)

☐ News object (1)

3 newss

Figure 7.3 – News admin page

For better readability in admin, we can customize what is displayed there – for example, if we want to display the headline for each news object instead. In /news/models.py, add the following function in bold:

```
from django.db import models

class News(models.Model):
    headline = models.CharField(max_length=200)
    body = models.TextField()
    date = models.DateField()

    def __str__(self):
        return self.headline
```

The __str__ method in Python represents the class objects as a string. __str__ will be called when the news objects are listed in admin. Note how readability is improved (as shown in *Figure 7.4*)!

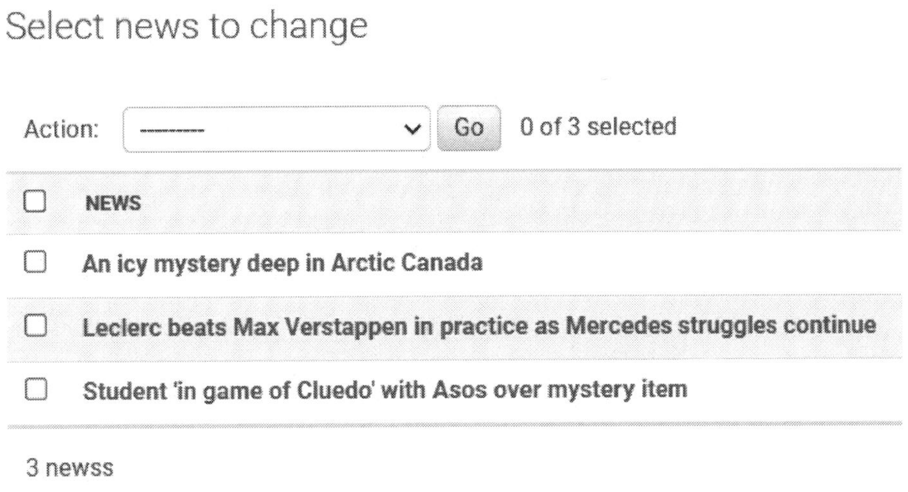

Select news to change

Action: [———— ▾] [Go]   0 of 3 selected

☐ **NEWS**

☐ **An icy mystery deep in Arctic Canada**

☐ **Leclerc beats Max Verstappen in practice as Mercedes struggles continue**

☐ **Student 'in game of Cluedo' with Asos over mystery item**

3 newss

Figure 7.4 – News admin page with headlines

Note that we don't need to do any migration, since no data is changed. We have just added a function that returns data.

Switching to a MySQL database

As we earlier mentioned, we are using SQLite throughout this book because it is the simplest. However, we will explain how to switch to a more robust database engine called MySQL.

> **Note**
> The book code will be based on SQLite, so the changes in this section are optional and won't be reflected either in the GitHub book repository or in upcoming chapters.

MySQL

MySQL is a popular open source SQL database management system developed by Oracle. There are several different ways of installing MySQL. For this section, we will install MySQL and a MySQL administration tool called phpMyAdmin. Both tools can be found in a development environment called XAMPP. So, let's install XAMPP.

XAMPP

XAMPP is a popular PHP development environment. XAMPP is a free Apache distribution containing MySQL, PHP, and Perl. XAMPP also includes phpMyAdmin. If you don't have XAMPP installed, go to `https://www.apachefriends.org/download.html`, download it, and install it.

Configuring the MySQL database

Execute XAMPP: 1) start the Apache Module, 2) start the MySQL module, and 3) click the MySQL **Admin** button (of the MySQL module), which will take us to the phpMyAdmin application (as shown in *Figure 7.5*):

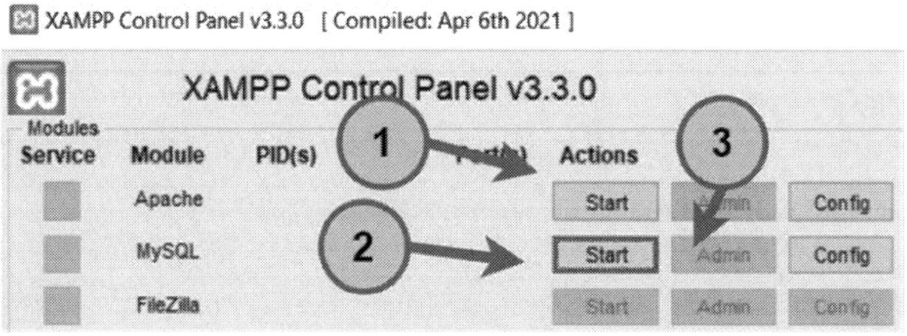

Figure 7.5 – Starting MySQL module in XAMPP

Over the phpMyAdmin application, enter your username and password. The default values are "root" (for the username) and an empty password (*Figure 7.6*):

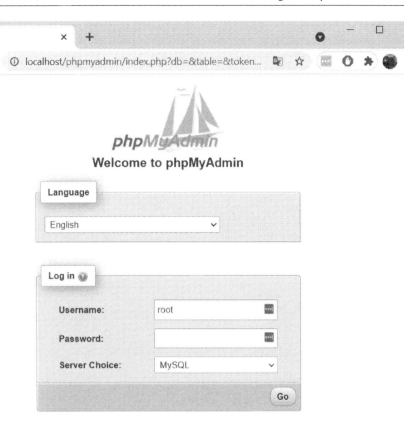

Figure 7.6 – XAMPP phpMyAdmin application

Once you have logged in to phpMyAdmin: 1) click the Databases tab, 2) enter the database name `moviereviews`, and 3) click the **Create** button (as shown in *Figure 7.7*).

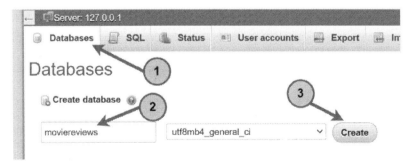

Figure 7.7 – Database creation

Configuring our project to use the MySQL database

First, we need to install a package called PyMySQL. PyMySQL is an interface for connecting to a MySQL database from Python. Go to the terminal and run the following commands:

- For macOS, run this:

```
pip3 install pymysql
```

- For Windows, run this:

```
pip install pymysql
```

Then, we need to add the following bold lines to the moviereviews/__init__.py file:

```
import pymysql
pymysql.install_as_MySQLdb()
```

This __init__.py file will be executed when we run the Django project, and the previous two lines import the PyMySQL package into the project.

Running the migrations

Since we switched the database, the new database is empty. First, we need to run the migrations again:

- For macOS, run this:

```
python3 manage.py migrate
```

- For Windows, run this:

```
python manage.py migrate
```

Then, we should see the tables in our phpMyAdmin application (as shown in *Figure 7.8*).

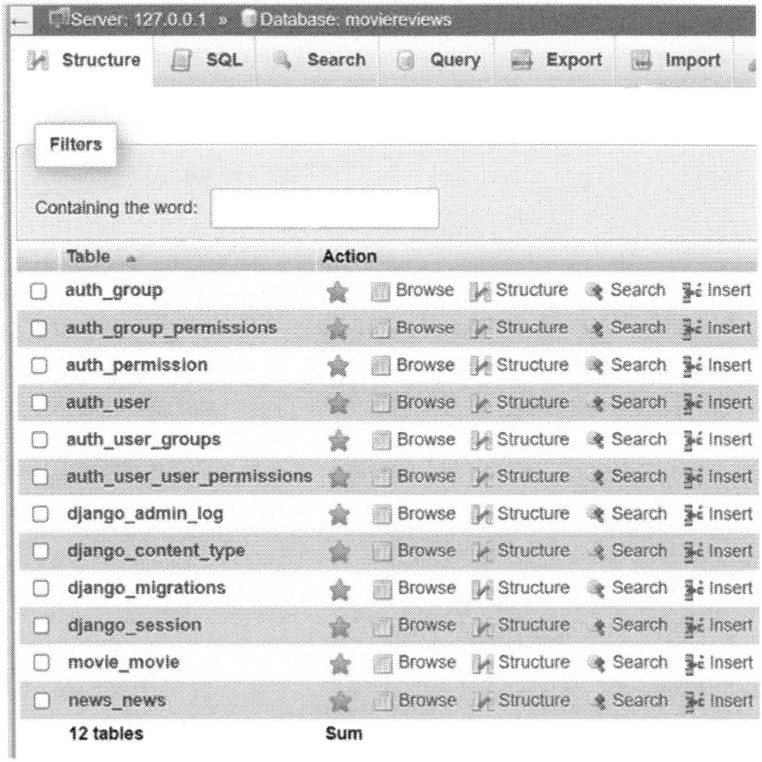

Figure 7.8 – The moviereviews database

Finally, we should repeat the process of creating a superuser and accessing the admin panel to create some movies and news.

Summary

We hope that you better understand how SQLite databases work and how Django supports database management. In the next chapter, we will define a base template to further improve the look and feel of our app.

8
Extending Base Templates

This chapter presents the concept of base templates and how they can be used to reduce duplicated template code. We will create a base template with a navbar and a footer and also add links to the different app pages.

In this chapter, we will be covering the following topics:

- Creating a base template
- Making the links work
- Adding a footer section
- Serving static files

Technical requirements

In this chapter, we will be using Python 3.8+. Additionally, we will be using the **VS Code** editor in this book, which you can download from `https://code.visualstudio.com/`.

The code for this chapter is located at `https://github.com/PacktPublishing/Django-4-for-the-Impatient/tree/main/Chapter08/moviereviewsproject`.

Creating a base template

We currently have our movies page, mailing list signup page, and news page. However, users have to manually enter in the URL to navigate to each of the pages, which is not ideal. Let's add a header bar that allows them to navigate between pages. We will begin with `movie/templates/home.html`:

1. We will use as a base the markup of the Navbar component from **getbootstrap** (`https://getbootstrap.com/docs/5.1/components/navbar/`). We also include the `bootstrap.bundle.min.js` script inside the `<head>` tag. This file provides additional user interface elements, such as dialog boxes, tooltips, carousels, and button interactions. Besides that, we will include a `meta viewport` tag that detects a user device and scales an application, depending on that device.

2. In `movie/templates/home.html`, make the following changes in bold:

```
<!DOCTYPE html>
<html>
  <head>
    ...
    <script src="https://cdn.jsdelivr.net/npm/
      bootstrap@5.1.1/dist/js/bootstrap.bundle.min.js"
      crossorigin="anonymous">
    </script>
    <meta name="viewport" content="width=device-width,
      initial-scale=1" />
  </head>

  <body>
    <nav class="navbar navbar-expand-lg navbar-light
      bg-light mb-3">
```

```
<div class="container">
  <a class="navbar-brand" href="#">Movies</a>
  <button class="navbar-toggler" type="button"
    data-bs-toggle="collapse"
    data-bs-target="#navbarNavAltMarkup"
    aria-controls="navbarNavAltMarkup"
    aria-expanded="false"
    aria-label="Toggle navigation">
    <span class="navbar-toggler-icon"></span>
  </button>
  <div class="collapse navbar-collapse"
    id="navbarNavAltMarkup">
    <div class="navbar-nav ms-auto">
      <a class="nav-link" href="#">News</a>
      <a class="nav-link" href="#">Login</a>
      <a class="nav-link" href="#">Sign Up</a>
    </div>
  </div>
</div>
</nav>

<div class="container">
...
```

We have added the navbar to home.html (as shown in *Figure 8.1*):

Figure 8.1 – Home page with navbar

We also included two links (**Login** and **Sign Up**), which will be used later.

If you reduce the browser window width, your navbar will respond accordingly (this is automatically provided by the Bootstrap elements we used, as shown in *Figure 8.2*):

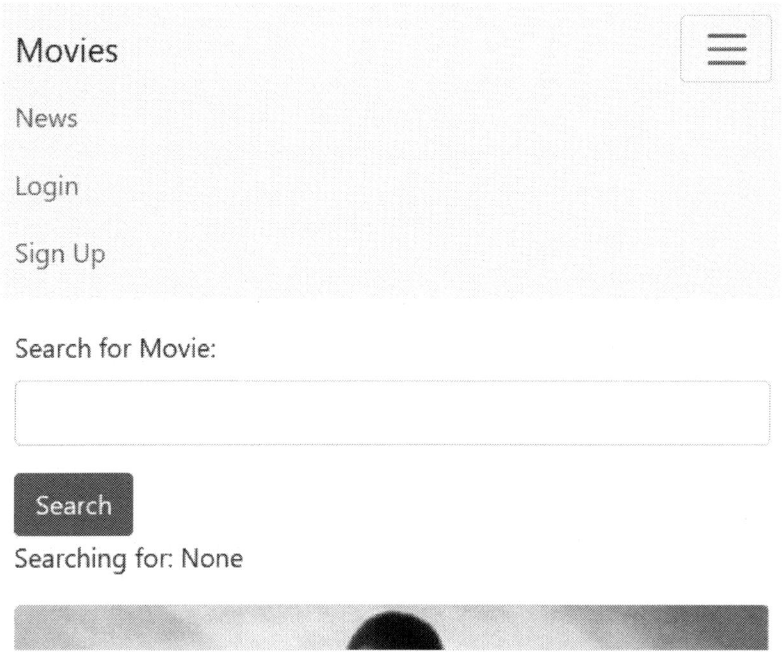

Figure 8.2 – Home page with navbar (reduced window width)

But should we repeat the same process and copy the exact same code into news . html and other future pages?

This would duplicate a lot of the same code. Worse, it will be very hard to maintain the code. Suppose we want to add a new link – we would have to add the link on multiple pages!

To fix this, we will be using base templates, where we can add the navbar to every single page. This allows us to make changes to our navbar in a single place, and it will apply to every page.

Since this will be a "global" template (which will be used across all pages and apps), we will add it to the main folder (moviereviews). In the moviereviews folder, create a folder called templates. In that folder, create a file, base.html. We will move the common HTML elements (such as the header and navbar) to the base. html file.

> **Note**
>
> We can name base.html anything, but using base.html is a common convention for base templates.

3. Fill moviereviews/templates/base.html with the following code:

```
<!DOCTYPE html>
<html>
  <head>
    <title>Movies App</title>
    <link href="https://cdn.jsdelivr.net/npm/
      bootstrap@5.1.1/dist/css/bootstrap.min.css"
      rel="stylesheet" crossorigin="anonymous" />
    <script src="https://cdn.jsdelivr.net/npm/
      bootstrap@5.1.1/dist/js/bootstrap.bundle.min.js"
      crossorigin="anonymous">
    </script>
    <meta name="viewport" content="width=device-width,
      initial-scale=1" />
  </head>

  <body>
    <nav class="navbar navbar-expand-lg
      navbar-light bg-light mb-3">
      <div class="container">
        <a class="navbar-brand" href="#">Movies</a>
        <button class="navbar-toggler" type="button"
          data-bs-toggle="collapse"
          data-bs-target="#navbarNavAltMarkup"
          aria-controls="navbarNavAltMarkup"
          aria-expanded="false"
          aria-label="Toggle navigation">
          <span class="navbar-toggler-icon"></span>
        </button>
        <div class="collapse navbar-collapse"
          id="navbarNavAltMarkup">
          <div class="navbar-nav ms-auto">
```

```
            <a class="nav-link" href="#">News</a>
            <a class="nav-link" href="#">Login</a>
            <a class="nav-link" href="#">Sign Up</a>
        </div>
      </div>
    </div>
  </nav>

  <div class="container">
    {% block content %}
    {% endblock content %}
  </div>
  </body>
</html>
```

Let's understand what is happening here.

base.html, as its name suggests, serves as the base for all pages. Thus, we include the header navbar in it. We will later include a footer section.

We then allocate a block where content can be slotted in from other child pages – for example, home.html and news.html:

```
    {% block content %}
    {% endblock content %}
```

This will become clear as we proceed.

4. Finally, we need to register the moviereviews/templates folder in our application settings. Make sure to add it to TEMPLATES DIRS in /moviereviews/settings.py:

```
...
TEMPLATES = [
    {
        'BACKEND': 'django.template.backends.django
          .DjangoTemplates',
        'DIRS': [os.path.join(BASE_DIR,
          'moviereviews/templates')],
        'APP_DIRS': True,
        ...
```

5. In `movie/templates/home.html`, we shouldn't have the header and navbar anymore. To simplify things, let's remove the sign-up mailing list form. Also, remove the `<div class="container">` tag, since it is loaded in the `base.html` template. The entire `movie/templates/home.html` will look something like this:

```
{% extends 'base.html' %}
{% block content %}
  <form action="">
    <div class="mb-3">
      <label class="form-label">Search for Movie:
      </label>
      <input type="text" name="searchMovie"
        class="form-control" />
    </div>
    <button type="submit" class="btn btn-primary">
      Search
    </button>
  </form>
  <p>Searching for: {{ searchTerm }}</p>
  <div class="row row-cols-1 row-cols-md-3 g-4">
    {% for movie in movies %}
    <div v-for="movie in movies" class="col">
      <div class="card">
        <img class="card-img-top" src="{{
          movie.image.url }}" />
        <div class="card-body">
          <h5 class="card-title fw-bold">{{
            movie.title }}</h5>
          <p class="card-text">{{ movie.description
            }}</p>
          {% if movie.url %}
          <a href="{{ movie.url }}"
            class="btn btn-primary">
            Movie Link
          </a>
          {% endif %}
```

```
                </div>
              </div>
            </div>
          {% endfor %}
        </div>
{% endblock content %}
```

Let's understand what is happening here.

base.html, as its name suggests, serves as the base for all pages. Thus, we include the header navbar in it. We will later include a footer section.

```
{% extends 'base.html' %}
```

With the extends tag, we extend from base.html by taking all the markup inside the block content tag in home.html and putting it into base.html (inside the block content section).

When you run the app and go to the home page, you should see the same site with the navbar included magically as before!

6.   Now, let's apply the preceding to news.html as well. Replace all existing content of /news/template/news.html with the following:

```
{% extends 'base.html' %}
{% block content %}
  {% for news in newss %}
  <div class="card mb-3">
    <div class="row g-0">
      <div>
        <div class="card-body">
          <h5 class="card-title">{{ news.headline
            }}</h5>
          <p class="card-text">{{ news.body }}</p>
          <p class="card-text"><small
            class="text-muted">
            {{ news.date }}
          </small></p>
        </div>
      </div>
    </div>
```

```
    </div>
    {% endfor %}
  {% endblock content %}
```

When you run your app, the news page should show the navbar as well (as shown in *Figure 8.3*):

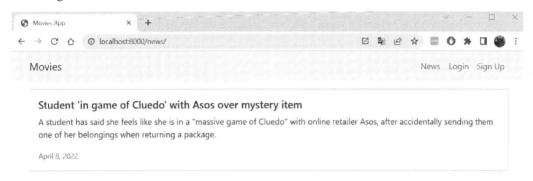

Figure 8.3 – News page extending the base.html template

Now, whenever you want to make a change to the navbar, you just have to do it once in `base.html`, and it will apply to all the pages!

Now, let's configure the header links.

Making the links work

The links in the navbar don't currently work. To enable them, in `moviereviews/templates/base.html`, add the following code in bold:

```
...
<body>
  <nav class="navbar navbar-expand-lg navbar-light
    bg-light mb-3">
    <div class="container">
      <a class="navbar-brand" href="{% url 'home' %}">
        Movies</a>
      <button class="navbar-toggler" type="button"
        data-bs-toggle="collapse"
        data-bs-target="#navbarNavAltMarkup"
        aria-controls="navbarNavAltMarkup"
        aria-expanded="false"
```

```
            aria-label="Toggle navigation">
            <span class="navbar-toggler-icon"></span>
        </button>
        <div class="collapse navbar-collapse"
          id="navbarNavAltMarkup">
          <div class="navbar-nav ms-auto">
            <a class="nav-link" href="{% url 'news' %}">
              News</a>
            <a class="nav-link" href="#">Login</a>
            <a class="nav-link" href="#">Sign Up</a>
          </div>
        </div>
      </nav>
    ...
```

When you run your app, the links will work. This is because we earlier defined the 'home' path in /moviereviews/urls.py:

```
...
urlpatterns = [
    path('admin/', admin.site.urls),
    path('', movieViews.home, name='home'),
    ...
```

We also defined the 'news' path in /news/urls.py:

```
...
urlpatterns = [
    path('', views.news, name='news'),
]
```

When you run your app now, you can navigate between the movie and news page using the links in the navbar.

Finally, let's include a footer section in our base.html template.

Adding a footer section

Let's add a footer section inside our base.html. In moviereviews/templates/base.html, we will make the following changes in bold:

```
...
    <div class="container">
      {% block content %}
      {% endblock content %}
    </div>

    <footer class="text-center text-lg-start bg-light
      text-muted mt-4">
      <div class="text-center p-4">
        © Copyright -
        <a class="text-reset fw-bold text-decoration-none"
          target="_blank"
          href="https://twitter.com/greglim81">
          Greg Lim
        </a> -
        <a class="text-reset fw-bold text-decoration-none"
          target="_blank"
          href="https://twitter.com/danielgarax">
          Daniel Correa
        </a>
      </div>
    </footer>
  </body>
</html>
```

The footer section displays a grey div in which we place the book authors' names, with links to their respective Twitter accounts. If you run the app now, it should give you something like *Figure 8.4*:

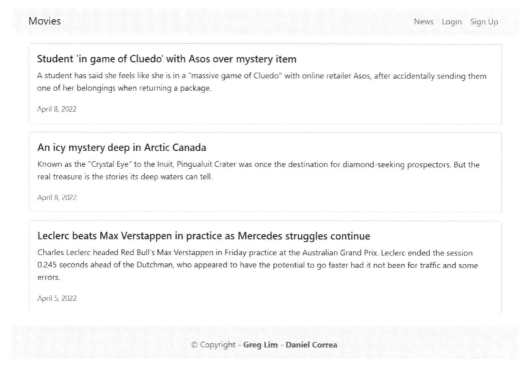

Figure 8.4 – News page

In the next section, we will look at how to display static images on our site.

Serving static files

Let's suppose we want to display an image icon for our site (as shown in *Figure 8.5*):

Figure 8.5 – A header with a static image icon

These are examples of fixed images on the site. These fixed images are static files. They are different from media files that users upload to the site, such as movie images.

In /moviereviews/settings.py, we have a STATIC_URL = '/static/'
property. Above the property is a comment, containing a link to documentation on how to
use static files:

```
...
# Static files (CSS, JavaScript, Images)
# https://docs.djangoproject.com/en/4.0/howto/static-files/


STATIC_URL = 'static/'
...
```

However, we will go through it here:

1. In /moviereviews, create a folder, static. In it, create an images folder to
    contain the fixed images used on our site.

2. Bring in an image file (for example, movie.png) that you want to display on your
    site into the images folder. In moviereviews/templates/base.html,
    replace the Movies link with the following:

    ```
    ...
        <body>
          <nav class="navbar navbar-expand-lg navbar-light
            bg-light mb-3">
            <div class="container">
              <a class="navbar-brand" href="{% url 'home'
                %}">
              {% load static %}
              <img src="{% static 'images/movie.png' %}"
                alt="" width="30" height="24"
                class="d-inline-block align-text-top" />
              Movies
            </a>
            ...
    ```

    We added an image to the navbar. To add static files to our template, we add the
    following line to the top of base.html, and because other templates inherit from
    base.html, we only have to add this once:

    ```
                {% load static %}
    ```

In the image source, we can then reference the static image:

```
<img src="{% static 'images/movie.png' %}" …
```

Since the `movie.png` image is not attached to a specific app (it is attached to the project folder), we need to include the `moviereviews/static` folder in the application settings.

3. Add at the end of the `/moviereviews/settings.py` file the following code in bold:

```
…


STATICFILES_DIRS = [
    BASE_DIR / 'moviereviews/static/',
]
```

Now, the brand image will be displayed in the navbar (as shown in *Figure 8.6*):

📽 Movies   News   Login   Sign Up

Figure 8.6 – The header with an icon

As well as images, you can link to other static file types – for example, PDF, CSS, and JavaScript files.

Summary

In this chapter, we learned how to create base templates that reduce duplicated code. We improved our application interface with the inclusion of a navbar and footer, and we learned how to manage static files. In the next chapter, we'll see how to navigate to a movie's detail page from the home page.

9
Creating a Movie Detail Page

Let's now go back to our movies app. In this chapter, we want to navigate to a movie's detail page when a user clicks on a movie title on the home page. We will create the movie URL, view, and template.

In this chapter, we will be covering the following topics:

- Creating a movie page
- Implementing links to individual movie pages

Technical requirements

In this chapter, we will be using Python 3.8+. Additionally, we will be using the **VS Code** editor in this book, which you can download from https://code.visualstudio.com/.

The code for this chapter is located at https://github.com/PacktPublishing/Django-4-for-the-Impatient/tree/main/Chapter09/moviereviewsproject.

Creating a movie page

Let's look at the steps:

1. First, we will add the movie details path in /moviereviews/urls.py:

    ```
    ...
    urlpatterns = [
        path('admin/', admin.site.urls),
        path('', movieViews.home, name='home'),
        path('about/', movieViews.about, name='about'),
        path('signup/', movieViews.signup, name='signup'),
        path('news/', include('news.urls')),
        path('movie/', include('movie.urls')),
    ]
    ...
    ```

    path('movie/', include('movie.urls')) will forward any requests with 'movie/' to the movie app's urls.py. We put all the paths related to the movie app in its own urls.py – that is, /movie/urls.py.

2. So, let's create the /movie/urls.py file with the following code:

    ```
    from django.urls import path
    from . import views

    urlpatterns = [
        path('<int:movie_id>', views.detail,
          name='detail'),
    ]
    ```

    The path shown in the previous code block is the primary key for the movie represented as an integer, <int:movie_id>. Remember that Django adds an auto-incrementing primary key to our database models under the hood.

    With this path, when a user comes to a URL – for example, localhost:8000/movie/4 – '4' is the integer (int) representing the movie ID. The URL matches path('movie/<int:movie_id>' and navigates to the detail page.

3. Next, in /movie/views.py, we add the def detail view:

    ```
    from django.shortcuts import render
    from django.http import HttpResponse
    ```

```
from django.shortcuts import get_object_or_404
from .models import Movie


...


def detail(request, movie_id):
    movie = get_object_or_404(Movie,pk=movie_id)
    return render(request, 'detail.html',
      {'movie':movie})
```

We use get_object_or_404 to get the specific movie object we want. We provide movie_id as the primary key, pk=movie_id. If there is a match, get_object_or_404, as its name suggests, returns us the object or the not found (404) object.

4. We then pass the movie object to detail.html. So, in /movie/templates/, create a file, detail.html. We will use the same Horizontal Card layout from news/templates/news.html and extend from base.html. The code in /movie/templates/detail.html will look like this:

```
{% extends 'base.html' %}
{% block content %}
<div class="card mb-3">
  <div class="row g-0">
    <div class="col-md-4">
      <img src="{{ movie.image.url }}"
        class="img-fluid rounded-start" alt="">
    </div>
    <div class="col-md-8">
      <div class="card-body">
        <h5 class="card-title">{{ movie.title }}</h5>
        <p class="card-text">{{ movie.description
          }}</p>
        <p class="card-text">
          {% if movie.url %}
            <a href="{{ movie.url }}"
              class="btn btn-primary">
              Movie Link
            </a>
```

```
        {% endif %}
      </p>
    </div>
  </div>
</div>
</div>
{% endblock content %}
```

We hope you are noticing the repeating pattern of creating a new view, URL and template.

5. If you visit a movie's detail URL, such as `localhost:8000/movie/1`, it will render the movie's details in its own page (as shown in *Figure 9.1*):

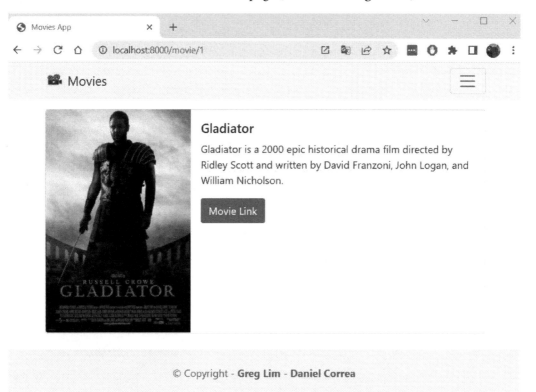

Figure 9.1 – Movie page

Later, in *Chapter 11*, *Letting Users Post, List, Update and Delete Movie Reviews*, we will add a Reviews section to the details page.

Implementing links to individual movie pages

Now that we have a movie's detail page, we will next implement the movie links to navigate to those detail pages from `/movie/templates/home.html`:

1. We simply wrap the movie title in `<a href...>`, as shown here in bold:

    ```
    ...
    {% for movie in movies %}
    <div v-for="movie in movies" class="col">
      <div class="card">
        <img class="card-img-top" src="{{
          movie.image.url }}" />
        <div class="card-body">
          <a href="{% url 'detail' movie.id %}">
            <h5 class="card-title fw-bold">{{
              movie.title }}</h5>
          </a>
          <p class="card-text">{{ movie.description }}
          </p>
          ...
    ```

    `{% url 'detail' movie.id %}` links to the detail path back in `/movie/urls.py`. Within the `{% ... %}` tag, we have specified the target name of our URL, `'detail'`, and also passed `movie.id` as a parameter.

2.   When you run your app now and go to the home page, the title will appear as a link to the detail page (as shown in *Figure 9.2*):

Gladiator

Gladiator is a 2000 epic historical drama film directed by Ridley Scott and written by David Franzoni, John Logan, and William Nicholson.

Movie Link

Fast & Furious 9

F9 (also known as F9: The Fast Saga and internationally as Fast & Furious 9) is a 2021 action film directed by Justin Lin from a screenplay by Daniel Casey and Lin.

Harry Potter and the Half-Blood Prince

Harry Potter and the Half-Blood Prince is a 2009 fantasy film directed by David Yates and distributed by Warner Bros. It is based on J. K. Rowling's 2005 novel of the same name.

Figure 9.2 – Home page with movie links

Summary

We have learned a lot so far! We have learned about databases, models, the admin interface, static files, media files, extending base templates, URLs, routing URLs, and much more. In this chapter, we added a movie detail page to our application. In the next chapter, we will learn how to allow a user to sign up and log in.

10
Implementing User Signup and Login

The next part of our app will concern user authentication where we allow users to sign up and log in. Implementing user authentication is famously hard. Fortunately, we can use Django's powerful, built-in authentication system that takes care of the many security pitfalls that can arise if we were to create our own user authentication from scratch.

In this chapter, we will be covering the following topics:

- Creating a signup form
- Creating a user
- Handling user creation errors
- Customizing UserCreationForm
- Showing whether a user is logged in
- Implementing the logout functionality
- Implementing the login functionality

Technical requirements

In this chapter, we will be using Python 3.8+. Additionally, we will be using the **VS Code** editor in this book, which you can download from `https://code.visualstudio.com/`.

The code for this chapter is located at `https://github.com/PacktPublishing/Django-4-for-the-Impatient/tree/main/Chapter10/moviereviewsproject`.

Creating a signup form

On our website, if users do not yet have an account, they will have to sign up for one first. So, let's look at how to create a signup account form:

1. Since a signup account doesn't belong to the movie or news app, let's create a dedicated app called `accounts` for it. In the Terminal, run the following:

    -   For macOS, run this:

        ```
        python3 manage.py startapp accounts
        ```

    -   For Windows, run this:

        ```
        python manage.py startapp accounts
        ```

2. Make sure to add the new app to `INSTALLED_APPS` in `/moviereviews/settings.py`:

    ```
    ...
    INSTALLED_APPS = [
        'django.contrib.admin',
        'django.contrib.auth',
        'django.contrib.contenttypes',
        'django.contrib.sessions',
        'django.contrib.messages',
        'django.contrib.staticfiles',
        'movie',
        'news',
        'accounts',
    ]
    ...
    ```

3. We will create a project-level URL for the accounts path in /moviereviews/ urls.py:

```
...
urlpatterns = [
    path('admin/', admin.site.urls),
    path('', movieViews.home, name='home'),
    path('about/', movieViews.about, name='about'),
    path('signup/', movieViews.signup, name='signup'),
    path('news/', include('news.urls')),
    path('movie/', include('movie.urls')),
    path('accounts/', include('accounts.urls')),
]
...
```

4. We will put all the paths related to the accounts app (for example, signup, login, and logout) in its own urls.py – that is, /accounts/urls.py (create this file with the following code):

```
from django.urls import path
from . import views

urlpatterns = [
    path('signupaccount/', views.signupaccount,
      name='signupaccount'),
]
```

5. Next, create def signupaccount in /accounts/views.py with the following code in bold:

```
from django.shortcuts import render
from django.contrib.auth.forms import UserCreationForm

def signupaccount(request):
    return render(request, 'signupaccount.html',
                {'form':UserCreationForm})
```

6. We will import `UserCreationForm`, which Django provides to easily create a signup form to register new users. Django forms are a vast topic in itself, and we will see how powerful they can be. We pass in the form to `signupaccount.html`.

7. Next, create `/accounts/templates/signupaccount.html` and simply fill in the following:

    ```
    {{ form }}
    ```

8. Run your app and go to `localhost:8000/accounts/signupaccount`. You will see a form with three fields – username, password1, and password2 (as shown in *Figure 10.1*):

Username: [   ]

Required. 150 characters or fewer. Letters, digits and @/./+/-/_ only. Password: [   ]

- Your password can't be too similar to your other personal information.
- Your password must contain at least 8 characters.
- Your password can't be a commonly used password.
- Your password can't be entirely numeric.

Password confirmation: [   ]
Enter the same password as before, for verification.

Figure 10.1 – Signup page

The form verifies that password1 and password2 match. The look of the form has much to be desired though.

9. Let's improve the styling by having `signupaccount.html` extend `base.html`. We will also wrap the fields in a `form` tag and have a **Submit** button. Replace the entire `/accounts/templates/signupaccount.html` with the following:

    ```
    {% extends 'base.html' %}
    {% block content %}
    <div class="card mb-3">
      <div class="row g-0">
        <div>
          <div class="card-body">
            <h5 class="card-title">Sign Up</h5>
            <p class="card-text">
              <form method="POST">
    ```

```
            {% csrf_token %}
            {{ form.as_p }}
            <button type="submit"
              class="btn btn-primary">
              Sign Up
            </button>
          </form>
        </p>
      </div>
    </div>
  </div>
</div>
{% endblock content %}
```

The form doesn't have an action, which means that it submits to the same page. We will show how this action is executed later in the *Creating a user* section. Note also that the form method is POST – that is, when the form submits, it sends a POST request, since we are sending data to the server. This is different from the signup mailing list form earlier where the form method is GET because we receive data from the signup form.

POST keeps the submitted information hidden from the URL. GET, in contrast, has the submitted data in the URL – for example, http://localhost:8000/signup/?email=greg%40greglim.com. Because the username and password are sensitive information, we want them hidden. A POST request will not put the information in the URL.

In general, we use POST requests for creation and GET requests for retrieval. There are also other requests, such as UPDATE, DELETE, and PUT, but they are more important for creating APIs.

There is a line, {% csrf_token %}. Django provides this to protect our form from **cross-site request forgery** (**CSRF**) attacks. You should use it for all your Django forms.

To output our form data, we use {{ form.as_p }}, which renders it within paragraph (<p>) tags.

10. When you run your site, the form will now look something like *Figure 10.2*:

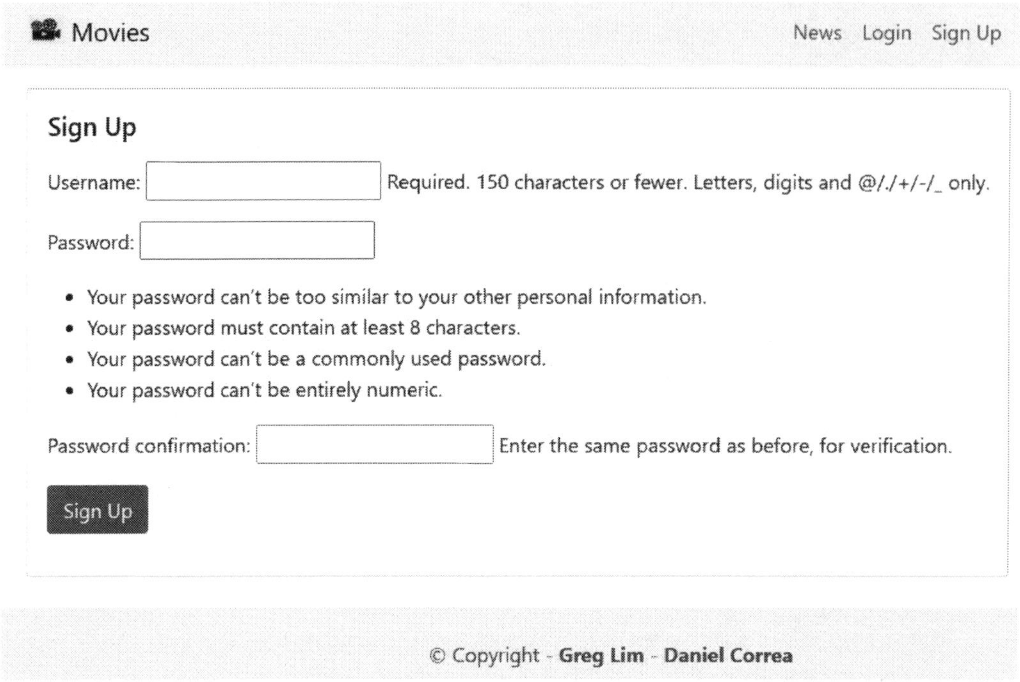

Figure 10.2 – Signup page

Now, let's see how to handle the request and create a user in admin when the user submits the signup form.

Creating a user

When the user submits the signup form, we will have to handle the request and create a user in admin. Use the following steps to do so:

1. Add the following in bold in `/accounts/views.py`:

```
from django.shortcuts import render
from django.contrib.auth.forms import UserCreationForm
from django.contrib.auth.models import User
from django.contrib.auth import login
from django.shortcuts import redirect


def signupaccount(request):
    if request.method == 'GET':
```

```
            return render(request, 'signupaccount.html',
                            {'form':UserCreationForm})
    else:
        if request.POST['password1'] ==
          request.POST['password2']:
            user = User.objects.create_user(
              request.POST['username'],
              password= request.POST['password1'])
            user.save()
            login(request, user)
            return redirect('home')
```

In def signupaccount, we first check whether the request received is a GET or POST request:

```
def signupaccount(request):
    if request.method == 'GET':
        return render(request, 'signupaccount.html',
                        {'form':UserCreationForm})
    else:
```

If it is a GET request, it means that it's a user navigating to the signup form via the localhost:8000/accounts/signupaccount URL, in which case we simply send them to signupaccount.html with the form.

But if it's a POST request, it means that it's a form submission to create a new user, so we move to the else block to create a new user.

In the else block, we ensure that the password entered in password1 and password2 are the same before going on to create the user:

```
    else:
        if request.POST['password1'] ==
          request.POST['password2']:
```

What are password1 and password2? If you look at the View Page Source markup for the form, you will see that the name for the password field is password1 and the name for the password confirmation field is password2. So, we first ensure that the password and confirm password values are the same before proceeding.

We then retrieve the data entered into the `username` field (`request.POST['username']`) and the `password1` field (`password=request.POST['password1']`):

```
user = User.objects.create_user(
    request.POST['username'],
    password= request.POST['password1'])
```

We pass in the data into `User.objects.create_user`, which helps us create the `user` object. But where did the `User` model come from? We did not create it. The `User` model is provided by Django's Auth app (`from django.contrib.auth.models import User`), which has the `User` model in the database set up for us. If you recall, in admin, we have **Users** (as shown in *Figure 10.3*), which contains the superuser account created for us when we ran `python3 manage.py createsuperuser`:

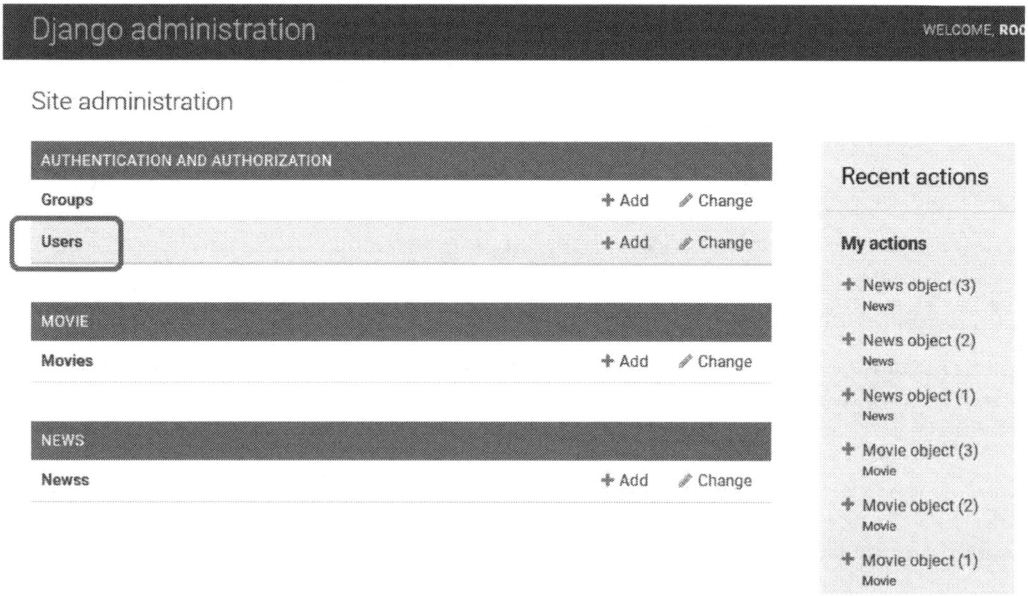

Figure 10.3 – Admin page

`user.save()` actually inserts the new user into the database:

```
user.save()
```

The newly added user will show up in `Users` in admin. After creating the user, we then log in with the new user:

```
login(request, user)
return redirect('home')
```

This means that, after someone signs up, we automatically log them in and redirect them to the home page.

2. Run your app now and go to `localhost:8000/accounts/signupaccount`. Create a user, and you will see the new user added to admin.

Now that we've built our signup form, let's see how we can resolve any errors that may arise while a user attempts to sign up.

Handling user creation errors

Let's improve the signup form to handle some errors.

Checking whether passwords do not match

What happens if `password1` doesn't match `password2`? To handle such an error, we add the following `else` block in bold in `/accounts/views.py`:

```
...

def signupaccount(request):
    if request.method == 'GET':
        return render(request, 'signupaccount.html',
                        {'form':UserCreationForm})
    else:
        if request.POST['password1'] ==
          request.POST['password2']:
            user = User.objects.create_user(
              request.POST['username'],
                        password=request.POST['password1'])
            user.save()
            login(request, user)
            return redirect('home')
        else:
            return render(request, 'signupaccount.html',
              {'form':UserCreationForm,
                'error':'Passwords do not match'})
```

If the passwords don't match, we render the user back to `signupaccount.html` and also pass in an error message, `Passwords do not match`.

But we also need to render the error message into `signupaccount.html`. In `/accounts/templates/signupaccount.html`, add the following code in bold:

```
{% extends 'base.html' %}
{% block content %}
<div class="card mb-3">
  <div class="row g-0">
    <div>
      <div class="card-body">
        <h5 class="card-title">Sign Up</h5>
        {% if error %}
        <div class="alert alert-danger mt-3" role="alert">
          {{ error }}
        </div>
        {% endif %}
        <p class="card-text">
        ...
```

First, we only show the error message if it exists:

```
{% if error %}
```

We render the error message in a bootstrap `alert` component:

```
<div class="alert alert-danger mt-3" role="alert">
  {{ error }}
</div>
```

This is so that a user can better notice the error and take the necessary corrective action (as shown in *Figure 10.4*):

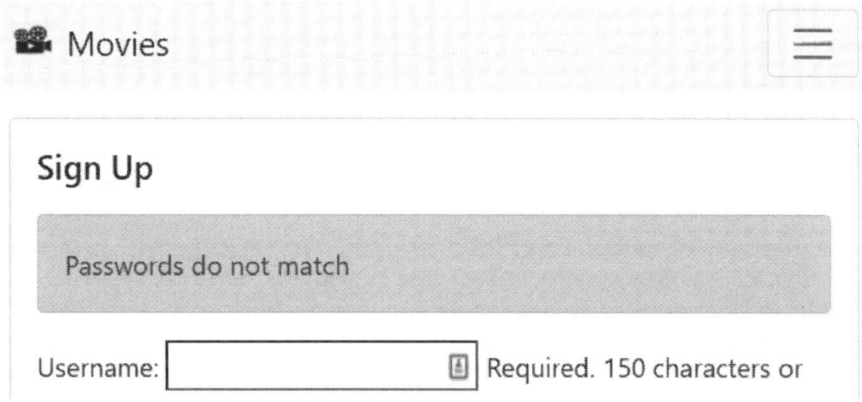

Figure 10.4 – Signup page with the passwords error

Checking if a username already exists

We have illustrated an example of how to handle errors that arise when a form is populated incorrectly. You can implement validation of other form data errors – for example, if a password length is less than eight characters.

There can be other kinds of errors that are identified only from a database – for example, if a user signs up with a username that already exists in the database. To catch such an error that is thrown by the database, we have to use `try` and `except`, as shown in bold here (include this code in `/accounts/views.py`):

```
...
from django.shortcuts import redirect
from django.db import IntegrityError

def signupaccount(request):
    if request.method == 'GET':
        return render(request, 'signupaccount.html',
                      {'form':UserCreationForm})
    else:
        if request.POST['password1'] ==
          request.POST['password2']:
            try:
                user = User.objects.create_user(
```

```
                        request.POST['username'],
                        password=request.POST['password1'])
                    user.save()
                    login(request, user)
                    return redirect('home')
                except IntegrityError:
                    return render(request,
                        'signupaccount.html',
                        {'form':UserCreationForm,
                        'error':'Username already taken. Choose
                            new username.'})
            else:
                return render(request, 'signupaccount.html',
                    {'form':UserCreationForm,
                    'error':'Passwords do not match'})
```

We will import `IntegrityError`, and using `try-except`, we will catch `IntegrityError` when it is thrown (in the case of a username already existing, as shown in *Figure 10.5*):

Sign Up

Username already taken. Choose new username.

Username: [   ] 🔒 Required. 150 characters or

Figure 10.5 – Signup page with a duplicated username error

Now, let's learn how to customize the `UserCreationForm`.

Customizing UserCreationForm

`UserCreationForm` currently shows quite a lot of extra help text (included by default), which is cluttering our form. We can actually customize `UserCreationForm`, which is a big topic on its own. Here, we will simply remove the default help text.

To customize the form, we have to create a new class that extends `UserCreationForm`. In `/accounts/`, create a new file called `forms.py` and fill it in with the following:

```python
from django.contrib.auth.forms import UserCreationForm


class UserCreateForm(UserCreationForm):
    def __init__(self, *args, **kwargs):
        super(UserCreateForm, self).__init__(*args,
                                             **kwargs)

        for fieldname in ['username', 'password1',
                          'password2']:
            self.fields[fieldname].help_text = None
            self.fields[fieldname].widget.attrs.update(
                {'class': 'form-control'})
```

Here, we have created a new form, `UserCreateForm`, which extends from `UserCreationForm`:

```python
class UserCreateForm(UserCreationForm):
```

In the form's constructor, `def __init__(self, *args, **kwargs):`, we call the super method:

```python
    def __init__(self, *args, **kwargs):
        super(UserCreateForm, self).__init__(*args,
            **kwargs)
```

We will also set `help_text` of the form's fields to `None` to remove them:

```python
        for fieldname in ['username', 'password1',
                          'password2']:
            self.fields[fieldname].help_text = None
            self.fields[fieldname].widget.attrs.update(
                {'class': 'form-control'})
```

And then we will set for each form field a `class` attribute to use a Bootstrap class.

Using UserCreateForm

Finally, in /accounts/views.py, change the following in bold to use
UserCreateForm instead of UserCreationForm:

```python
from django.shortcuts import render
from django.contrib.auth.forms import UserCreationForm
from .forms import UserCreateForm
from django.contrib.auth.models import User
...


def signupaccount(request):
    if request.method == 'GET':
        return render(request, 'signupaccount.html',
                        {'form':UserCreateForm})
    else:
        if request.POST['password1'] ==
          request.POST['password2']:
            try:
                user = User.objects.create_user(
                  request.POST['username'],
                  password=request.POST['password1'])
                user.save()
                login(request, user)
                return redirect('home')
            except IntegrityError:
                return render(request,
                  'signupaccount.html',
                  {'form':UserCreateForm,
                  'error':'Username already taken. Choose
                  new username.'})
        else:
            return render(request, 'signupaccount.html',
              {'form':UserCreateForm,
                'error':'Passwords do not match'})
```

When you go to the signup account form, the help text will not be there, and the input will have a new style (*Figure 10.6*):

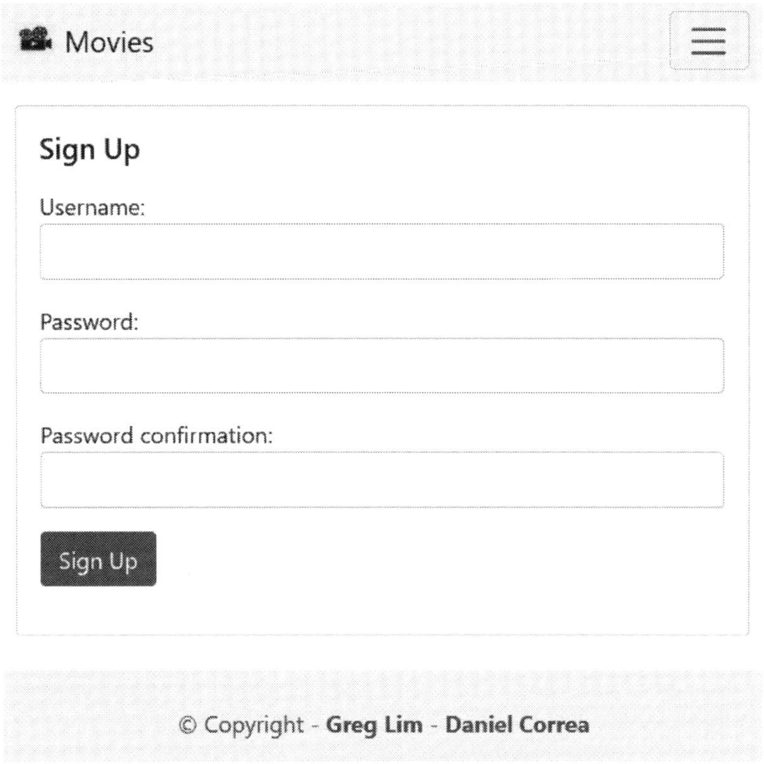

Figure 10.6 – Signup page with UserCreateForm

In the next section, we will show the proper navigation links, depending if the user is logged or not.

Showing whether a user is logged in

After a user has signed up and logged in, we are still showing the **Login** and **Sign Up** buttons in the navbar (as shown in *Figure 10.7*):

Figure 10.7 – The navbar for the logged in user

For logged-in users, we should be hiding these buttons and showing the **Logout** button instead. To do so, let's go to our base template. Remember that our base template is the starting point for everything, and we extend it to the different views.

In `moviereviews/templates/base.html`, add the following code in bold:

```
...
<nav class="navbar navbar-expand-lg navbar-light
  bg-light mb-3">
  ...
    <div class="collapse navbar-collapse"
      id="navbarNavAltMarkup">
    <div class="navbar-nav ms-auto">
      <a class="nav-link" href="{% url 'news' %}">
        News</a>
      {% if user.is_authenticated %}
        <a class="nav-link" href="#">
          Logout ({{ user.username }})
        </a>
      {% else %}
        <a class="nav-link" href="#">Login</a>
        <a class="nav-link" href="#">Sign Up</a>
      {% endif %}
      </div>
    </div>
  ...
```

Note that we have a `user` object, which Django automatically provides (via the installed auth app) and passes in for us:

```
{% if user.is_authenticated %}
  <a class="nav-link" href="#">
    Logout ({{ user.username }})
  </a>
{% else %}
```

The user object contains the `username`, `password`, `email`, `first_name`, and `last_name` properties. Additionally, we can check whether a user is logged in with `{% if user.is_authenticated %}`.

If a user is authenticated, we render a **Logout** button with the corresponding username, `{{ user.username }}`. Otherwise, it means that the user is not logged in, and we show the **Login** and **Sign Up** buttons.

Implementing the logout functionality

Create the logout path in `/accounts/urls.py` with the following in bold:

```
...
urlpatterns = [
     path('signupaccount/', views.signupaccount,
name='signupaccount'),
     path('logout/', views.logoutaccount,
        name='logoutaccount'),
]
```

In `/accounts/views.py`, implement the `logoutaccount` function with the following in bold:

```
...
from django.contrib.auth.models import User
from django.contrib.auth import login, logout
from django.shortcuts import redirect
from django.db import IntegrityError

...

def logoutaccount(request):
    logout(request)
    return redirect('home')
```

We simply call `logout` and `redirect` to go back to the home page.

We then need to have `<a href>` in the logout button call the logout path. We also have the signup button call the `signupaccount` path. So, in `moviereviews/templates/base.html`, add the following in bold:

```
...
    <nav class="navbar navbar-expand-lg navbar-light
        bg-light mb-3">
```

```
...
        <div class="collapse navbar-collapse"
            id="navbarNavAltMarkup">
          <div class="navbar-nav ms-auto">
            <a class="nav-link" href="{% url 'news' %}">
              News</a>
            {% if user.is_authenticated %}
              <a class="nav-link"
                href="{% url 'logoutaccount' %}">
                Logout ({{ user.username }})
              </a>
            {% else %}
              <a class="nav-link" href="#">Login</a>
              <a class="nav-link"
                href="{% url 'signupaccount' %}">
                Sign Up
              </a>
            {% endif %}
          </div>
        </div>
...
```

When you are logged in, you can now log out by clicking on the **Logout** button (as shown in *Figure 10.8*):

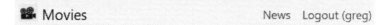

Figure 10.8 – The navbar with the Logout button implemented

Implementing the login functionality

Having implemented signup and logout, let's now implement login:

1. Create a login path in /accounts/urls.py:

```
...
urlpatterns = [
    path('signupaccount/', views.signupaccount,
      name='signupaccount'),
```

```
        path('logout/', views.logoutaccount,
          name='logoutaccount'),
        path('login/', views.loginaccount,
          name='loginaccount'),
    ]
```

2. In /accounts/views.py, implement loginaccount with the following in bold:

```
...

...
from django.contrib.auth.models import User
from django.contrib.auth.forms import
  AuthenticationForm
from django.contrib.auth import login, logout,
    authenticate
...


def loginaccount(request):
    if request.method == 'GET':
        return render(request, 'loginaccount.html',
                      {'form':AuthenticationForm})
    else:
        user = authenticate(request,
          username=request.POST['username'],
          password=request.POST['password'])
        if user is None:
            return render(request,'loginaccount.html',
                      {'form': AuthenticationForm(),
                       'error': 'username and password do
                            not match'})
        else:
            login(request,user)
            return redirect('home')
```

loginaccount will be similar to signupaccount:

```
def loginaccount(request):
    if request.method == 'GET':
```

```
        return render(request, 'loginaccount.html',
                    {'form':AuthenticationForm})
```

We first handle the case where the request is a GET request – that is, the user clicks on Login on the navbar – and we render loginaccount.html. We then pass in AuthenticationForm. Much like UserCreationForm for signup, Django provides AuthenticationForm to quickly get a login form up and running:

```
    else:
        user = authenticate(request,
            username=request.POST['username'],
            password=request.POST['password'])
        if user is None:
            return render(request,'loginaccount.html',
                    {'form': AuthenticationForm(),
                    'error': 'username and password do
                            not match'})
        else:
            login(request,user)
            return redirect('home')
```

If the request type is not GET (the user submits the login form and sends a POST request), we proceed to authenticate the user with the values they entered in the username and password fields.

If the user returned from authenticate is None – that is, we are unable to find an existing user with the supplied username/password – we return the user to loginaccount.html with the 'username and password do not match' error.

Otherwise, it means the authentication is successful, and we log in the user and redirect them to the home page:

/accounts/templates/loginaccount.html

3. Create the new file, accounts/templates/loginaccount.html, copy the markup from accounts/templates/signupaccount.html, and change the labeling from 'Sign Up' to 'Login':

```
{% extends 'base.html' %}
{% block content %}
<div class="card mb-3">
```

```html
  <div class="row g-0">
    <div>
      <div class="card-body">
        <h5 class="card-title">Login</h5>
        {% if error %}
        <div class="alert alert-danger mt-3"
          role="alert">
          {{ error }}
        </div>
        {% endif %}
        <p class="card-text">
          <form method="POST">
            {% csrf_token %}
            {{ form.as_p }}
            <button type="submit"
              class="btn btn-primary">
                Login
            </button>
          </form>
        </p>
      </div>
    </div>
  </div>
</div>
{% endblock content %}
```

4. Finally, in moviereviews/templates/base.html, we set href for loginaccount:

```html
      ...
          {% if user.is_authenticated %}
            <a class="nav-link" href="{% url
              'logoutaccount' %}">
              Logout ({{ user.username }})
            </a>
          {% else %}
            <a class="nav-link"
```

```
            href="{% url 'loginaccount' %}">
            Login
        </a>
        <a class="nav-link"
            href="{% url 'signupaccount' %}">
            Sign Up
        </a>
    {% endif %}
...
```

Our navbar is now complete and fully functioning. For users not logged in, the navbar will show the login and signup links. When a user logs in, the navbar will show only the **Logout** button.

Summary

In this chapter, we implemented a complete authentication system. Now, users can sign up, log in, and log out. We also learned how to take advantage of the Django User model, `AuthenticationForm`, and `UserCreationForm`, and we even learned how to extend some of those classes.

In the next chapter, we will implement a complete movie review system.

11
Letting Users Create, Read, Update, and Delete Movie Reviews

Now that we have implemented the authentication system, it is time to let logged-in users perform the standard CRUD operations on reviews for movies.

In this chapter, we will be covering the following topics:

- Letting users post movie reviews
- Creating a review
- Listing reviews
- Updating a review
- Deleting a review
- Implementing authorization

Technical requirements

In this chapter, we will be using Python 3.8+. Additionally, we will be using the **VS Code** editor in this book, which you can download from `https://code.visualstudio.com/`.

The code for this chapter is located at `https://github.com/PacktPublishing/Django-4-for-the-Impatient/tree/main/Chapter11/moviereviewsproject`.

Letting users post movie reviews

We will now implement letting logged-in users post reviews for movies. We have to first create a Review model:

1. In `movie/models.py`, add the following to define a Review model:

    ```
    from django.db import models
    from django.contrib.auth.models import User
    ...


    class Review(models.Model):
        text = models.CharField(max_length=100)
        date = models.DateTimeField(auto_now_add=True)
        user =
          models.ForeignKey(User,on_delete=models.CASCADE)
        movie = models.ForeignKey(
          Movie,on_delete=models.CASCADE)
        watchAgain = models.BooleanField()


        def __str__(self):
            return self.text
    ```

    The `text` field stores the review text:

    ```
    text = models.CharField(max_length=100)
    ```

    For the review `date`, we specify `auto_now_add=True`:

    ```
    date = models.DateTimeField(auto_now_add=True)
    ```

    This means that, when someone creates this object, the current datetime will be automatically filled in.

> **Note**
> This makes the field non-editable. Once the datetime is set, it is fixed.

For the user and movie fields, we are using ForeignKey, which allows for a many-to-one relationship:

```
user =
   models.ForeignKey(User,on_delete=models.CASCADE)
movie = models.ForeignKey(
   Movie,on_delete=models.CASCADE)
```

This means that user can create multiple reviews. Similarly, movie can have multiple reviews.

For user, the reference is to the built-in User model that Django provides for authentication. For all many-to-one relationships such as ForeignKey, we must also specify an on_delete option. This means that when you remove a user or movie, for instance, its associated reviews will be deleted as well. Note that this does not apply in the other direction – that is, when you remove a review, the associated movie and user still remain:

```
watchAgain = models.BooleanField()
```

Lastly, we have a Boolean property, watchAgain, for users to indicate whether they will watch the movie again.

2. To have our Review model appear in the admin dashboard, remember that we have to register it by adding the following in bold into /movie/admin.py:

```
from django.contrib import admin
from .models import Movie, Review


admin.site.register(Movie)
admin.site.register(Review)
```

3. In the terminal, make the migration for the new model and apply the changes to the sqlite3 database:

- For macOS, use these:

```
python3 manage.py makemigrations
python3 manage.py migrate
```

- For Windows, use these:

```
python manage.py makemigrations
python manage.py migrate
```

Now, let's see how to let users post reviews on movies from the site.

Creating a review

We have seen how to create model objects from the admin – for example, creating a `movie` object. But how do we allow users to create their own objects, such as letting them post a review from the site? After all, not everyone should have access to the admin panel.

Let's create a page for them to do so:

1. We first create a path in /movie/urls.py:

    ```
    from django.urls import path
    from . import views

    urlpatterns = [
        path('<int:movie_id>', views.detail,
          name='detail'),
        path('<int:movie_id>/create', views.createreview,
            name='createreview'),
    ]
    ```

/movie/views.py

2. In /movie/views.py, add `def createreview`:

    ```
    ...
    from django.shortcuts import get_object_or_404, redirect
    from .models import Movie, Review
    from .forms import ReviewForm


    ...


    def createreview(request, movie_id):
        movie = get_object_or_404(Movie,pk=movie_id)
    ```

```
        if request.method == 'GET':
            return render(request, 'createreview.html',
                            {'form':ReviewForm(), 'movie':
                                movie})
        else:
            try:
                form = ReviewForm(request.POST)
                newReview = form.save(commit=False)
                newReview.user = request.user
                newReview.movie = movie
                newReview.save()
                return redirect('detail',
                    newReview.movie.id)
            except ValueError:
                return render(request,
                    'createreview.html',
                    {'form':ReviewForm(),'error':'bad data
                        passed in'})
```

We first get the movie object from the database:

```
    movie = get_object_or_404(Movie,pk=movie_id)
```

When we receive a GET request, it means that a user is navigating to the create review page, and we render createreview.html and pass in the review form for the user to create the review:

```
    if request.method == 'GET':
        return render(request, 'createreview.html',
                        {'form':ReviewForm(), 'movie':
                            movie})
```

We will show in *step 6* how to create the review form. When the user submits the createreview form, this function will receive a POST request, and we enter the else clause:

```
    else:
        try:
```

We retrieve the submitted form from the request:

```
        form = ReviewForm(request.POST)
```

We create and save a new review object from the form's values but do not yet put it into the database (`commit=False`) because we want to specify the user and movie relationships for the review:

```
newReview = form.save(commit=False)
```

Finally, we specify the user and movie relationships for the review and save the review into the database:

```
newReview.user = request.user
newReview.movie = movie
newReview.save()
return redirect('detail',
  newReview.movie.id)
```

We then redirect the user back to the movie's detail page. If there's any error with the passed-in data, we render `createreview.html` again and pass in an error message:

```
except ValueError:
    return render(request,
      'createreview.html',
      {'form':ReviewForm(),'error':'bad data
        passed in'})
```

Next, let's create the `createreview.html` page.

/movie/templates/createreview.html

3. In `/movie/templates`, create a new file, `createreview.html`, with the following code:

```
{% extends 'base.html' %}
{% block content %}
<div class="card mb-3">
  <div class="row g-0">
    <div>
      <div class="card-body">
        <h5 class="card-title">Add Review for {{
          movie.title }}</h5>
        {% if error %}
        <div class="alert alert-danger mt-3"
```

```
        role="alert">
        {{ error }}
      </div>
      {% endif %}
      <p class="card-text">
        <form method="POST">
          {% csrf_token %}
          {{ form.as_p }}
          <button type="submit"
            class="btn btn-primary">
            Add Review
          </button>
        </form>
      </p>
    </div>
  </div>
</div>
</div>
{% endblock content %}
```

As you can see, createreview.html is very similar to the other pages. So, let's move ahead and see how to create the review form.

4. To create the review form, we can make use of ModelForm provided by Django to automatically create forms from models. In /movie, create the forms.py file and fill it with the following code:

```
from django.forms import ModelForm, Textarea
from .models import Review

class ReviewForm(ModelForm):
    def __init__(self, *args, **kwargs):
        super(ModelForm, self).__init__(*args,
          **kwargs)
        self.fields['text'].widget.attrs.update(
          {'class': 'form-control'})
        self.fields['watchAgain'].widget.attrs.update(
```

```
            {'class': 'form-check-input'})

    class Meta:
        model = Review
        fields = ['text','watchAgain']
        labels = {
            'watchAgain': ('Watch Again')
        }
        widgets = {
            'text': Textarea(attrs={'rows': 4}),
        }
```

We need to inherit from `ModelForm`:

```
class ReviewForm(ModelForm):
```

Similar to what we did with `UserCreationForm`, we set some Bootstrap classes for our form fields:

```
def __init__(self, *args, **kwargs):
    super(ModelForm, self).__init__(*args,
        **kwargs)
    self.fields['text'].widget.attrs.update(
        {'class': 'form-control'})
    self.fields['watchAgain'].widget.attrs.update(
        {'class': 'form-check-input'})
```

We then specify which model the form is for and the fields we want in the form:

```
class Meta:
    model = Review
    fields = ['text','watchAgain']
```

In our case, our review form will need just the `text` and `watchAgain` fields. Recall the following from our Review model:

```
class Review(models.Model):
    text = models.CharField(max_length=100)
    date = models.DateTimeField(auto_now_add=True)
    user = models.ForeignKey(
      User,on_delete=models.CASCADE)
    movie = models.ForeignKey(
```

```
        Movie,on_delete=models.CASCADE)
    watchAgain = models.BooleanField()
```

`date` is auto-populated, and `user` and `movie` are already provided. Thus, we need only the user to input the `text` and `watchAgain` fields in the form:

```
        labels = {
            'watchAgain': ('Watch Again')
        }
```

We have a `labels` object where we can create custom labels for each of our fields. For example, we want to display `'Watch Again'` instead of `'watchAgain'` (our users are not programmers!).

By default, `CharField` is displayed as input text. We override this default field (with the use of widgets) to have `Textarea` for our text field:

```
        widgets = {
            'text': Textarea(attrs={'rows': 4}),
        }
```

Note

For more information about `ModelForms`, you can check out the Django documentation at `https://docs.djangoproject.com/en/4.0/topics/forms/modelforms/`.

/movie/templates/detail.html

5. Finally, we render an `Add Review` button on the movie details page (`/movie/templates/detail.html`) with the following codes in bold:

```
    ...
        <div class="card-body">
          <h5 class="card-title">{{ movie.title }}</h5>
          <p class="card-text">{{ movie.description
            }}</p>
          <p class="card-text">
            {% if movie.url %}
              <a href="{{ movie.url }}"
                class="btn btn-primary">
                Movie Link
```

```
        </a>
    {% endif %}
    {% if user.is_authenticated %}
    <a href="{% url 'createreview' movie.id %}"
       class="btn btn-primary">
       Add Review
    </a>
    {% endif %}
  </p>
</div>
...
```

Note that we have enclosed the Add Review link in an if user.is_ authenticated block. This is to ensure that we only allow logged-in users to add a review. Users who are not logged in will not see the Add Review link.

6.   Log in, go to a movie, and click **Add Review** (*Figure 11.1*):

Figure 11.1 – The movie page with the Add Review button

You will see the review form that Django automatically generated for you (*Figure 11.2*):

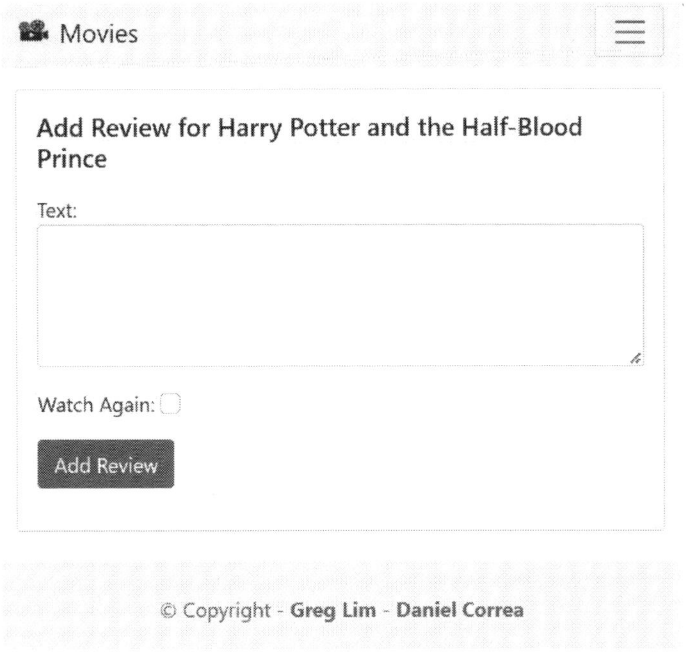

Figure 11.2 – The review page

After adding the review, you can check the admin panel where it will be reflected. Next, we will see how to list reviews on the movie details page.

Listing reviews

Now, we want to list a movie's reviews on the movie details page (*Figure 11.3*):

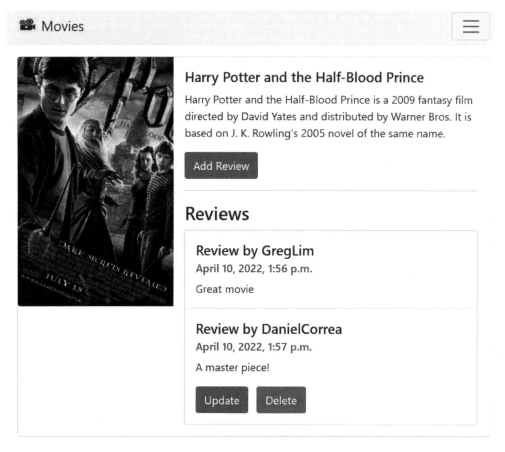

Figure 11.3 – The movie page with reviews

Let's look at the steps to do so:

1. In /movie/views.py, in def detail, add the following code in bold:

```
...
def detail(request, movie_id):
    movie = get_object_or_404(Movie,pk=movie_id)
    reviews = Review.objects.filter(movie = movie)
    return render(request, 'detail.html',
                    {'movie':movie, 'reviews': reviews})
...
```

Let's see what's happening in the code. Using the `filter` function, we retrieve reviews for a particular movie only:

```
reviews = Review.objects.filter(movie = movie)
```

We then pass in the reviews to `detail.html`:

```
return render(request, 'detail.html',
              {'movie':movie, 'reviews': reviews})
```

/movie/templates/detail.html

2. We list the reviews under the movie's card component (in `/movie/templates/detail.html`) by adding the section in bold:

```
...
<div class="card-body">
  <h5 class="card-title">{{ movie.title }}</h5>
  <p class="card-text">{{ movie.description
    }}</p>
  <p class="card-text">

    ...

  </p>
  <hr />
  <h3>Reviews</h3>
  <ul class="list-group">
  {% for review in reviews %}
    <li class="list-group-item pb-3 pt-3">
      <h5 class="card-title">
        Review by {{ review.user.username }}
      </h5>
      <h6 class="card-subtitle mb-2 text-muted">
        {{ review.date }}
      </h6>
      <p class="card-text">{{ review.text }}</p>
      {% if user.is_authenticated and user ==
        review.user %}
      <a class="btn btn-primary me-2"
        href="#">Update</a>
      <a class="btn btn-danger"
```

```
        href="#">Delete</a>
      {% endif %}
    </li>
  {% endfor %}
  </ul>
</div>
...
```

Using a for loop, we render a Bootstrap list group item component for each review
(https://getbootstrap.com/docs/5.1/components/list-group/):

```
<ul class="list-group">
{% for review in reviews %}
  <li class="list-group-item pb-3 pt-3">

    ...
  </li>
{% endfor %}
</ul>
```

We render username, the review date and the review text:

```
<h5 class="card-title">
  Review by {{ review.user.username }}
</h5>
<h6 class="card-subtitle mb-2 text-muted">
  {{ review.date }}
</h6>
<p class="card-text">{{ review.text }}</p>
```

We also check whether a user is logged in, and if a review belongs to the user,
render the update and delete link to allow them to update/delete it:

```
{% if user.is_authenticated and user ==
  review.user %}
<a class="btn btn-primary me-2"
  href="#">Update</a>
<a class="btn btn-danger"
  href="#">Delete</a>
{% endif %}
```

Otherwise, we hide the update/delete links, so that a user can only update/delete reviews they have posted. They can't do so for others' reviews.

3. On the movie details page, you will be able to see the reviews for a movie now. If you are logged in, you can see the update and delete buttons for reviews you posted (*Figure 11.4*):

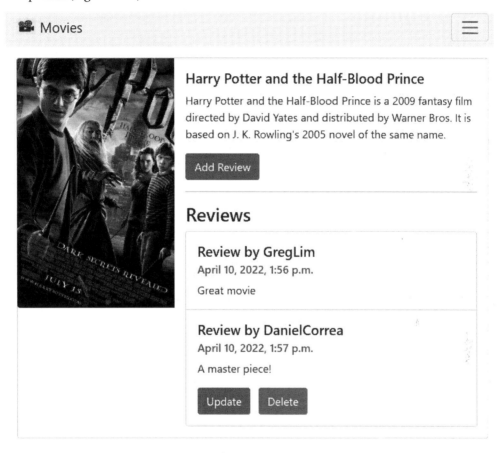

Figure 11.4 – The movie page with reviews

When you log out, you can't see them anymore. Let's continue with updating a review.

Updating a review

Let's look at the steps to do this:

1. We create a URL path to update a review in /movie/urls.py:

    ```
    ...
    urlpatterns = [
        path('<int:movie_id>', views.detail,
          name='detail'),
        path('<int:movie_id>/create', views.createreview,
            name='createreview'),
        path('review/<int:review_id>', views.updatereview,
            name='updatereview'),
    ]
    ```

    The path takes in the review ID (the review's primary key) – for example, http://
    localhost:8000/movie/review/2.

2. In /movie/views.py, we then add def updatereview:

    ```
    ...

    def updatereview(request, review_id):
        review = get_object_or_404(
          Review,pk=review_id,user=request.user)
        if request.method == 'GET':
            form = ReviewForm(instance=review)
            return render(request, 'updatereview.html',
                            {'review': review,'form':form})
        else:
            try:
                form = ReviewForm(request.POST,
                    instance=review)
                form.save()
                return redirect('detail', review.movie.id)
            except ValueError:
                return render(request,
                    'updatereview.html',
    ```

```
                 {'review': review,'form':form,
                  'error':'Bad data in form'})
```

We first retrieve the `review` object with the review ID:

```
        review = get_object_or_404(
          Review,pk=review_id,user=request.user)
```

We also supply the logged-in user to ensure that other users can't access the review – for example, if they manually enter the URL path in the browser. Only the user who created this review can update/delete it.

If the request type is GET, it means they navigated to the page from the movie details page:

```
        if request.method == 'GET':
            form = ReviewForm(instance=review)
            return render(request, 'updatereview.html',
                          {'review': review,'form':form})
```

Thus, we render `ReviewForm` we used previously in creating a review, but this time, we pass the review object into the form so that the form's fields will be populated with the object's values, ready for the user to edit. See how Django's `ModelForm` saves us so much work!

In the `else` block, the request type is POST, which means the user is trying to submit the update form.

```
        else:
            try:
                form = ReviewForm(request.POST,
                  instance=review)
                form.save()
                return redirect('detail', review.movie.id)
```

We retrieve the values from the form and do `form.save()` to update the existing review. We then redirect back to the movie details page.

If there is a problem with the content the user has provided, we catch it with the `ValueError` exception:

```
            except ValueError:
                return render(request,
                'updatereview.html',
```

```
{'review': review,'form':form,
    'error':'Bad data in form'})
```

/movie/templates/updatereview.html

3. We create a new file, `/movie/templates/updatereview.html`, and fill it with the following:

```
{% extends 'base.html' %}
{% block content %}
<div class="card mb-3">
  <div class="row g-0">
    <div>
      <div class="card-body">
        <h5 class="card-title">
          Update Review for {{ review.movie.title }}
        </h5>
        {% if error %}
        <div class="alert alert-danger mt-3"
          role="alert">
          {{ error }}
        </div>
        {% endif %}
        <p class="card-text">
          <form method="POST">
            {% csrf_token %}
            {{ form.as_p }}
            <button type="submit"
              class="btn btn-primary">
              Update Review
            </button>
          </form>
        </p>
      </div>
    </div>
  </div>
</div>
```

```
</div>
{% endblock content %}
```

Again, the preceding markup is similar to the other template files. See how Django greatly simplifies template and form creation for us!

/movie/templates/detail.html

4. Lastly, back in /movie/templates/detail.html, we add the 'updatereview' URL to the update button with the following in bold:

```
...

                {% if user.is_authenticated and user ==
                    review.user %}
                <a class="btn btn-primary me-2"
                    href="{% url 'updatereview' review.id
                        %}">
                    Update
                </a>
                <a class="btn btn-danger"
                    href="#">Delete</a>
                {% endif %}

...
```

5. When we run our app and try to update a review, the form will appear, and it will be filled with the existing review's values (*Figure 11.5*):

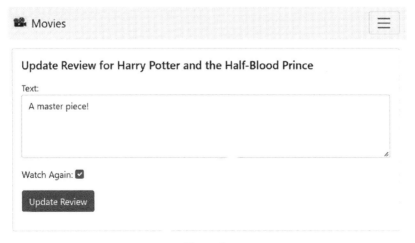

Figure 11.5 – The update review page

Update the review with the new values, and upon submitting the form, the updated review will be reflected on the movie details page.

Deleting a review

Having implemented the update of a review, let's now implement deleting a review:

1. Create a new path to delete a review in /movie/urls.py (you should be familiar with this by now):

```
...
urlpatterns = [
    path('<int:movie_id>', views.detail,
        name='detail'),
    path('<int:movie_id>/create', views.createreview,
        name='createreview'),
    path('review/<int:review_id>', views.updatereview,
        name='updatereview'),
    path('review/<int:review_id>/delete',
        views.deletereview,
        name='deletereview'),
]
```

2. In /movie/views.py, add def deletereview:

```
...


def deletereview(request, review_id):
    review = get_object_or_404(Review, pk=review_id,
        user=request.user)
    review.delete()
    return redirect('detail', review.movie.id)
```

You can see that deletereview is quite straightforward. We get the review object and call its delete method. As with update, we supply the logged-in user to ensure that only the user who created this review can delete it. We then redirect back to the movie's detail page.

3. Back in the listing of reviews on the movie details page (/movie/templates/ detail.html), we now add the deletereview URL:

```
...
            {% if user.is_authenticated and user ==
              review.user %}
            <a class="btn btn-primary me-2"
              href="{% url 'updatereview' review.id
                %}">
              Update
            </a>
            <a class="btn btn-danger"
              href="{% url 'deletereview' review.id
                %}">
              Delete
            </a>
            {% endif %}
...
```

When you run your app now, log in and go to a specific movie, you will be able to delete reviews you have posted.

Implementing authorization

We have implemented authentication where we allow users to sign up and log in. But we also need authorization that authorizes access to certain pages only to logged-in users.

Currently, if a user manually enters the URL to create a review – for example, http:// localhost:8000/movie/2/create – they can still access the form. We should authorize access to creating/updating/deleting reviews only to logged-in users. We will also authorize access to logout.

Let's look at the steps to do so:

1. We import and add the @login_required decorator to the views that we want to authorize, as shown in bold:

/movie/views.py

```
...
from .forms import ReviewForm
```

```
from django.contrib.auth.decorators import
  login_required

...


@login_required
def createreview(request, movie_id):

    ...


@login_required
def updatereview(request, review_id):

    ...


@login_required
def deletereview(request, review_id):

    ...
```

/accounts/views.py

```
...

from django.db import IntegrityError
from django.contrib.auth.decorators import
  login_required

...


@login_required
def logoutaccount(request):

    ...
```

2. We also have to add at the end of /moviereviews/settings.py the following:

```
...



LOGIN_URL = 'loginaccount'
```

This redirects a user (who is not logged in) to the login page when they attempt to access an authorized page.

When you run your app now, ensure that you are logged out and go to the create review page – for example, `http://localhost:8000/movie/2/create` – where you will be redirected to the login page.

Summary

We have now finished our movie application. We implemented a complete CRUD system for movie reviews. Now, users can create, list, update, and delete reviews. We also learned how to manage the application authorization, and we limited access for not-logged-in users to some routes and methods.

In the next chapter, we will learn how to deploy our application to the cloud.

12

Deploying the Application to the Cloud

Our project is currently running on our local machine. To get our site live on the real, public internet for the world to use, we need to deploy it onto an actual server. A popular way to do so is to deploy our Django project on PythonAnywhere, as it is free to use for small websites. Let's see how to deploy our application to the cloud.

In this chapter, we will be covering the following topics:

- Managing GitHub and Git
- Cloning our code onto PythonAnywhere
- Configuring virtual environments
- Setting up your web app
- Configuring static files
- Changing db.sqlite3 to MySQL or PostgresSQL

Technical requirements

In this chapter, we will be using Python 3.8+. We will be using **Git** to upload our code to the cloud, which you can download from `https://git-scm.com/downloads`. Finally, we will be using the **VS Code** editor in this book, which you can download from `https://code.visualstudio.com/`.

Managing GitHub and Git

To get our code on sites such as PythonAnywhere, we need our code to be on a code-sharing site such as GitHub or Bitbucket. In this chapter, we will use GitHub. If you are already familiar with uploading your code to GitHub, please skip the following section. Otherwise, you can follow along.

Let's look at the steps:

1. Go to `https://github.com` and sign up for an account if you don't have one. To put your project on GitHub, you will need to create a repository for it to live in. Create a new repository by clicking on + at the top-right and select **New repository** (*Figure 12.1*):

Figure 12.1 – GitHub – create a new repository option

2. Give your repository a name such as `moviereviews`. Select the **Public** radio box and hit **Create repository** (*Figure 12.2*):

Create a new repository

A repository contains all project files, including the revision history. Already have a project repository elsewhere? Import a repository.

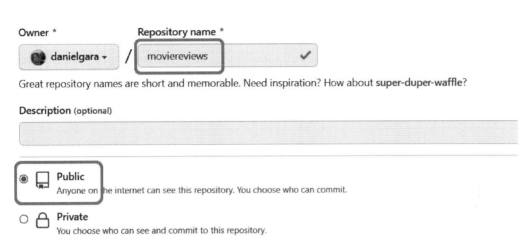

Owner *

danielgara ▾   /   movietreviews   ✓

Great repository names are short and memorable. Need inspiration? How about **super-duper-waffle**?

Description (optional)

⦿ 🖥 **Public**
Anyone on the internet can see this repository. You choose who can commit.

○ 🔒 **Private**
You choose who can see and commit to this repository.

Figure 12.2 – GitHub – create a new repository

3. We will begin to move our code onto GitHub. In your local machine's Terminal, ensure you have Git installed by running the following:

```
git
```

4. When you run `git` in the terminal, if you see Git usage and commands listed, you have Git installed (*Figure 12.3*):

```
PS C:\Users\yo> git
usage: git [--version] [--help] [-C <path>] [-c <name>=<value>]
           [--exec-path[=<path>]] [--html-path] [--man-path] [--info-path]
           [-p | --paginate | -P | --no-pager] [--no-replace-objects] [--bare]
           [--git-dir=<path>] [--work-tree=<path>] [--namespace=<name>]
           <command> [<args>]
```

Figure 12.3 – Executing git command in Terminal

If you don't see them, you will need to install Git. Visit the Git site (`https://git-scm.com/downloads`) and follow the instructions to install Git. When Git is installed, you might need to close and reopen the Terminal and in it type `git` to ensure that it is installed.

Now, what is Git? Git is a version control for projects and is very popular in the development world. It allows us to have save points (Git calls them `commits`) in our code. If we make mistakes in our project at any point in time, we can go back to previous save points when the project is working. Git also allows multiple developers to work on the project together without worrying about one overwriting the code of another.

5. Let's upload our code to GitHub. In the `moviereviewsproject` folder, enter the following:

```
git init
```

`git init` marks your folder as a Git project where you can begin to track changes. A hidden folder, `.git`, is added to the project folder. The `.git` folder stores all the objects and refs that Git uses and creates as part of your project's history.

6. Next, run the following:

```
git add .
```

This adds everything in your project to the staging environment to prepare a snapshot before committing it to the official history.

7. Go ahead to commit them by running the following:

```
git commit -m "first version"
```

This creates a save point in your code. You can identify different commits by the descriptive messages you provide.

8. Next, run the following:

```
git branch -M main
```

We create a branch called `main`. This will be the place in which we store our application code.

Next, we want to save our Git project on GitHub.

9. In the repository page in GitHub, copy the `git remote add origin`
    `<your-origin-path>` command (*Figure 12.4*) and run it in the Terminal
    (remember to replace `<your-origin-path>` with yours):

...or create a new repository on the command line

```
echo "# moviereviews" >> README.md
git init
git add README.md
git commit -m "first commit"
git branch -M main
git remote add origin https://github.com/danielgara/moviereviews.git
git push -u origin main
```

Figure 12.4 – Locating your origin path

This creates a new connection record to the remote repository:

```
git remote add origin <your-origin-path>
```

10. To move the code from your local computer to GitHub, run the following:

```
git push -u origin main
```

If the upload is successful, you should see a message like this (*Figure 12.5*):

```
Enumerating objects: 96, done.
Counting objects: 100% (96/96), done.
Delta compression using up to 12 threads
Compressing objects: 100% (89/89), done.
Writing objects: 100% (96/96), 692.02 KiB | 16.09 MiB/s, done.
Total 96 (delta 16), reused 0 (delta 0), pack-reused 0
remote: Resolving deltas: 100% (16/16), done.
To https://github.com/danielgara/moviereviews.git
 * [new branch]      main -> main
Branch 'main' set up to track remote branch 'main' from 'origin'.
```

Figure 12.5 – A successful git push to the GitHub repository

> **Note**
>
> If this is your first time uploading code to GitHub, you will probably see
> a prompt, asking you to log in to GitHub. Please complete that process.

The previous command pushes the code to GitHub. When you reload the GitHub repository page, your project's code will be reflected there (*Figure 12.6*):

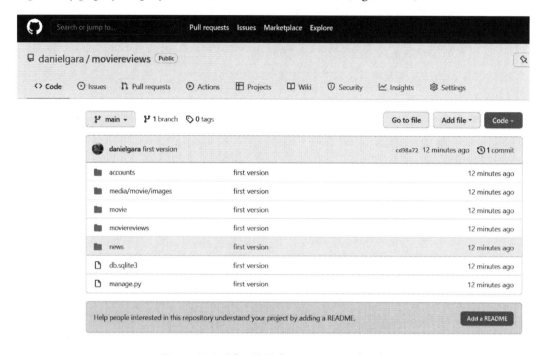

Figure 12.6 – The GitHub repository updated

> **Note**
> Do note that there is much more to Git and GitHub. We have just covered the necessary steps to upload our code to GitHub.

With this, we have now gotten our code on GitHub. Next, we will clone our code on PythonAnywhere.

Cloning our code on to PythonAnywhere

PythonAnywhere is a web-hosting service (https://www.pythonanywhere.com/). You can host, run, and code Python in the cloud. It also offers some free services, which we will use.

The steps to deploy an existing Django project on PythonAnywhere can be found at `https://help.pythonanywhere.com/pages/DeployExistingDjangoProject/`, but I will go through them with you here.

Now that we have our code on GitHub, we will have PythonAnywhere retrieve our code from there:

1. First, create a beginner free account in PythonAnywhere here: `https://www.pythonanywhere.com/registration/register/beginner/`.

2. In PythonAnywhere, click on **Dashboard | New console | $ Bash** to access its Linux Terminal (*Figure 12.7*):

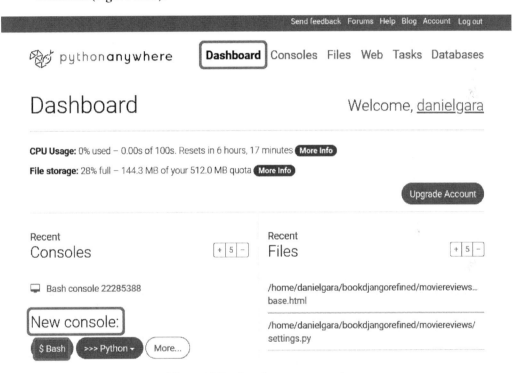

Figure 12.7 – Creating a new console

3. This will open a Bash console. Back in your GitHub repository, click on **Code** and copy the URL to clone (*Figure 12.8*):

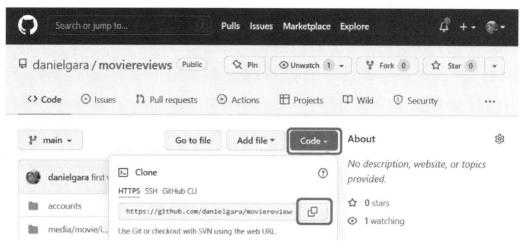

Figure 12.8 – Copying the GitHub repository URL

4. To clone, back in the PythonAnywhere Bash shell, run `git clone <repo-url>` – for example (`git clone https://github.com/danielgara/moviereviews.git`):

```
git clone <repo-url>
```

This will take all your code from the GitHub repository and clone it in PythonAnywhere. When the clone completes, you can do `'ls'` in Bash, and you will see a folder with the repository name (which contains the repository code) (*Figure 12.9*).

 Bash console 23981828

```
15:57 ~ $ git clone https://github.com/danielgara/moviereviews.git
Cloning into 'moviereviews'...
remote: Enumerating objects: 96, done.
remote: Counting objects: 100% (96/96), done.
remote: Compressing objects: 100% (73/73), done.
remote: Total 96 (delta 16), reused 96 (delta 16), pack-reused 0
Unpacking objects: 100% (96/96), 692.00 KiB | 28.00 KiB/s, done.
Updating files: 100% (79/79), done.
15:58 ~ $ ls
README.txt  moviereviews
15:58 ~ $ 
```

Figure 12.9 – Checking with the ls command that the repository was successfully cloned

Configuring virtual environments

Virtual environments are used to create separate development environments for different projects with different requirements. For example, you can specify which version of Python and which libraries/modules you want to be installed in a particular virtual environment.

As an example, to create a virtual environment in the PythonAnywhere bash, we could run the following:

```
mkvirtualenv -p python3.8 <environment name>
```

Here, we have specified that we use Python 3.8 in `virtualenv`. Whatever packages we install will always be there and independent of other `virtualenvs`.

Now, in the PythonAnywhere bash, run the following:

```
mkvirtualenv -p python3.8 moviereviewsenv
```

We will see the name of `virtualenv` in Bash, which means we are in the **Virtual Environment** (**VE**) (*Figure 12.10*).

Figure 12.10 – Bash located in virtualenv

Back in our `virtualenv`, we need to install `django` and `pillow` (as we did in development). So, run the following:

```
pip install django pillow
```

You should see a message like this (*Figure 12.11*):

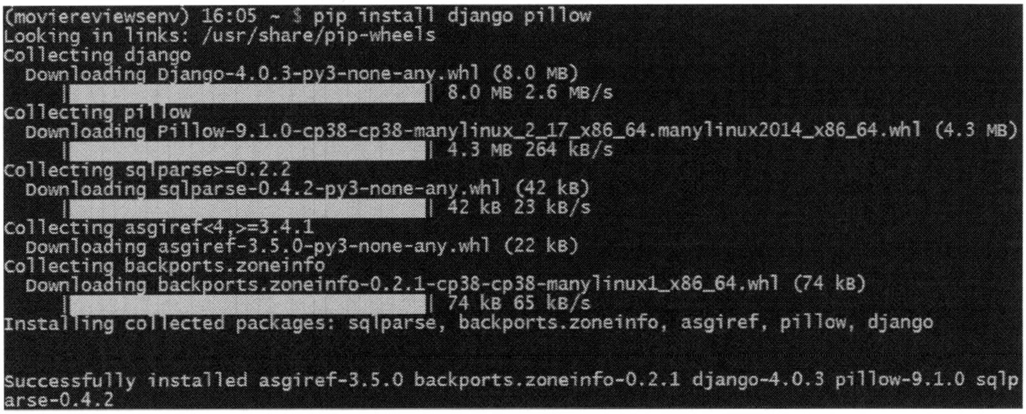

Figure 12.11 – Django and pillow installed

Setting up your web app

At this point, you need to be ready with three pieces of information:

- The path to your Django project's top folder – the folder that contains "manage.py". A simple way to get this is to type pwd in your project folder in Bash – for example, /home/danielgara/moviereviews/.

- The name of your project (the name of the folder that contains your settings.py) – for example, moviereviews.

- The name of your virtualenv – for example, moviereviewsenv.

Let's look at how we can create a web app with a manual config:

1. In your browser, open a new tab and go to the PythonAnywhere dashboard. Click on the **Web** tab (*Figure 12.12*):

Figure 12.12 – The PythonAnywhere Web tab

2. Click **Add a new web app**. Under **Select a Python Web framework**, choose **Manual configuration** (*Figure 12.13*):

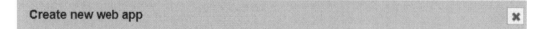

Select a Python Web framework

...or select "Manual configuration" if you want detailed control.

- » **Django**
- » **web2py**
- » **Flask**
- » **Bottle**
- » **Manual configuration** (including virtualenvs)

What other frameworks should we have here? Send us some feedback using the link at the top of the page!

Figure 12.13 – Selecting Manual configuration

> **Note**
> Make sure you choose **Manual configuration**, not the **Django** option; that's for new projects only.

3. Select the right version of Python (the same one you used to create your virtualenv). In our case, it was `Python 3.8`. Finally, click **Next**.

4. Once the web app is created, you need to enter the name of your virtualenv in the **Virtualenv** section (*Figure 12.14*). You can just use its short name, `moviereviewsenv`, and it will automatically complete its full path in `/home/username/.virtualenvs`:

Virtualenv:

Use a virtualenv to get different versions of flask, django etc from our default system ones. More info here. You need to **Reload your web app** to activate it; NB - will do nothing if the virtualenv does not exist.

/home/danielgara/.virtualenvs/moviereviewsenv

↻ Start a console in this virtualenv

Figure 12.14 – Entering the virtualenv name

5. Next, enter the path to your project folder in the **Code** section, both for **Source code** and **Working directory** (*Figure 12.15*):

Code:

What your site is running.

Source code:

/home/danielgara/
➡Go to directory

Working directory:

/home/danielgara/
➡Go to directory

Figure 12.15 – Entering the path to your code

6. Click the `wsgi.py` file inside the **Code** section – not the one in your local Django project folder (*Figure 12.16*):

Code:

What your site is running.

Source code:

/home/danielgara/
➤Go to directory

Working directory:

/home/danielgara/
➤Go to directory

WSGI configuration file:

/var/www/danielgara_pythonanywhere_com_wsgi.py

Figure 12.16 – Accessing the wsgi.py file

It will take you to an editor where you can change it.

7. Delete everything except the Django section and uncomment that section. Your WSGI file will look something like the following:

```
# +++++++++++ DJANGO +++++++++++
# To use your own django app use code like this:
import os
import sys

path = '/home/danielgara/moviereviews'
if path not in sys.path:
    sys.path.append(path)

os.environ['DJANGO_SETTINGS_MODULE'] =
    'moviereviews.settings'

from django.core.wsgi import import get_wsgi_application
application = get_wsgi_application()
```

Be sure to substitute the correct path to your project, the folder that contains the `manage.py` file:

```
path = '/home/danielgara/moviereviews'
```

Make sure you put the correct value for DJANGO_SETTINGS_MODULE (where the settings.py file is located):

```
os.environ['DJANGO_SETTINGS_MODULE'] =
    'moviereviews.settings'
```

Finally, save the file.

8. At any point you want to get out of the virtualenv, you can run deactivate in the Bash. To get back to a virtualenv, you should run the following:

```
workon <virtualenv-name>.
```

9. Next, we need to add to the allowed hosts in settings.py. Go to the PythonAnywhere **Files** tab and navigate through the source code directory (*Figure 12.17*):

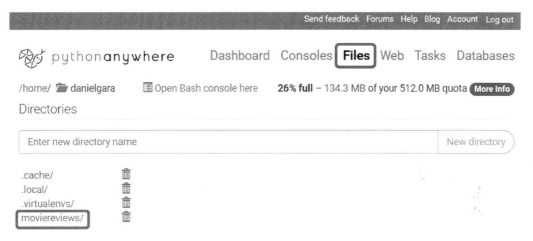

Figure 12.17 – Accessing the source code directory

10. Then, go to the moviereviews/ folder and click on the settings.py file. In settings.py, modify the ALLOWED_HOSTS variable:

```
...
# SECURITY WARNING: don't run with debug turned on in
    production!
DEBUG = True


ALLOWED_HOSTS = ['*']

...
```

Save the file.

11. Then, go to the **Web** tab and hit the Reload button for your domain (*Figure 12.18*):

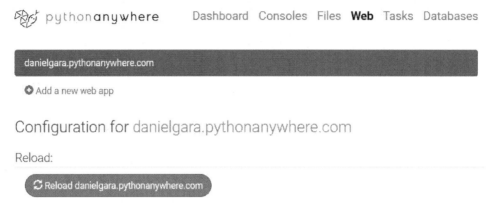

Figure 12.18 – Reloading the web app

The ALLOWED_HOSTS settings represent which host/domain names our Django site can serve. This is a security measure to prevent HTTP Host header attacks. We used the asterisk (*) wildcard to indicate that all domains are acceptable. In your production projects, you can explicitly list which domains are allowed.

12. Go to your project's URL (it is the blue link in the previous screenshot) and the home page should now appear (*Figure 12.19*):

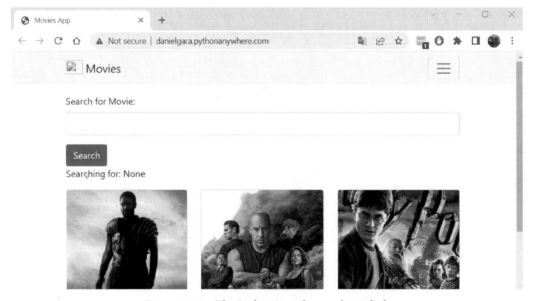

Figure 12.19 – The PythonAnywhere web app link

We are almost there! However, note that the static images are still not showing. Let's fix that in the next section.

Configuring static files

Let's fix the problem of our static and media images not showing:

1. In settings.py (on the PythonAnywhere website), we have to add the following in bold:

```
...
STATIC_URL = 'static/'
STATIC_ROOT = os.path.join(BASE_DIR,'static')

# Default primary key field type
# https://docs.djangoproject.com/en/4.0/ref/settings/
#default-auto-field

DEFAULT_AUTO_FIELD = 'django.db.models.BigAutoField'

MEDIA_ROOT = os.path.join(BASE_DIR,'media')
MEDIA_URL = '/media/'
...
```

The STATIC_ROOT variable defines a central location into which we collect all static files.

2. Save the file and back in the bash console (inside the virtualenv), go to the moviereviews folder (where the manage.py file is located):

```
cd moviewreviews/
```

Execute the following command (*Figure 12.20*):

```
python manage.py collectstatic
```

This command collects all your static files from each of your app folders (including the static files for the admin app) and from any other folders you specify in `settings.py` and copies them into `STATIC_ROOT`:

```
(moviereviewsenv) 18:14 ~ $ cd moviereviews/
(moviereviewsenv) 18:14 ~/moviereviews (main)$ ls
accounts  db.sqlite3  manage.py  media  movie  moviereviews  news
(moviereviewsenv) 18:14 ~/moviereviews (main)$ python manage.py collectstatic

129 static files copied to '/home/danielgara/moviereviews/static'.
(moviereviewsenv) 18:16 ~/moviereviews (main)$
```

Figure 12.20 – Executing the python manage.py collectstatic command

You need to rerun this command whenever you want to publish new versions of your static files.

3. Next, set up a static file mapping to get our web servers to serve out your static files for you. In the **Web** tab on the PythonAnywhere dashboard, under **Static files**, enter the same URL as `STATIC_URL` in the URL section (typically, `/static/`).

4. Enter the path from `STATIC_ROOT` into the path section (as shown in *Figure 12.21* – the full path, including `/home/username/moviereviews/static`):

Static files:

Files that aren't dynamically generated by your code, like CSS, JavaScript or uploaded files, can be served much faster straight off the disk if you specify them here. You need to **Reload your web app** to activate any changes you make to the mappings below.

URL	Directory	Delete
/static/	/home/danielgara/moviereviews/static	🗑

Figure 12.21 – Defining the static files

5. Then, on the **Web** tab, hit **Reload**, and your static images should appear on your site now (*Figure 12.22*):

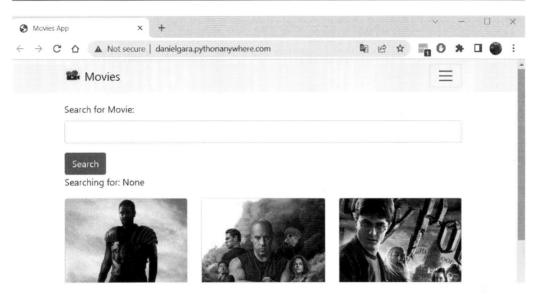

Figure 12.22 – The Movies app – home page

Set DEBUG to False

For local development, we have set DEBUG=True. This shows us the detailed error description and from which line of code it is resulting from. We should however hide these in production (we don't want to expose all our secrets out in the open) by setting DEBUG=False.

This can be done by going to the PythonAnywhere dashboard, going to your project's settings.py, and setting DEBUG=False. Then, save it and reload the web app.

.gitignore

We can ignore some files when uploading a production project to GitHub – for example, the __pycache__ directory, which is created automatically when Django runs the .py files. We should also ignore the db.sqlite3 file (since it contains all our movies, reviews, and user data). And if you are using a Mac, we can ignore .DS_Store, which stores information about folder settings on macOS.

To ignore those files, we must create a .gitignore file in the project root folder. Remember to do this when you are working with real projects. The final .gitignore will look like the following:

```
__pycache__/
db.sqlite3
.DS_Store
```

Changing db.sqlite3 to MySQL or PostgresSQL

Our current database is set to SQLite, which works fine for small projects. But when the project or the data size grows, we want to switch to other databases such as MySQL or PostgreSQL.

PythonAnywhere allows free usage of MySQL, but for PostgreSQL, you will need to have a paid account.

To start using MySQL, you can refer to PythonAnywhere's brief and useful documentation (https://help.pythonanywhere.com/pages/UsingMySQL/). You will need to recreate some of the steps you took in *Chapter 7, Understanding the Database*, in the *Switching to a MySQL database* section.

> **Note**
>
> After you have set up MySQL or any other database because it's a brand new database, you will have to create a new superuser (python manage.py createsuperuser) and run the makemigrations/migrate command:
>
> python manage.py makemigrations
>
> python manage.py migrate

Summary

We have gone through quite a lot of content to equip you with the skills to create a Django full stack app. We have covered the major features of Django, templates, views, URLs, user authentication, authorization, models, and deployment. You now have the knowledge to go and build your own websites with Django. The CRUD functionality in our Reviews app is common in many web applications – for example, you already have all the tools to create a blog, to-do list, or shopping cart web applications.

Hopefully, you have enjoyed this book and would like to learn more from us.

Index

U

V

W

X

Packt.com

Subscribe to our online digital library for full access to over 7,000 books and videos, as well as industry leading tools to help you plan your personal development and advance your career. For more information, please visit our website.

Why subscribe?

- Spend less time learning and more time coding with practical eBooks and Videos from over 4,000 industry professionals

- Improve your learning with Skill Plans built especially for you

- Get a free eBook or video every month

- Fully searchable for easy access to vital information

- Copy and paste, print, and bookmark content

Did you know that Packt offers eBook versions of every book published, with PDF and ePub files available? You can upgrade to the eBook version at packt.com and as a print book customer, you are entitled to a discount on the eBook copy. Get in touch with us at customercare@packtpub.com for more details.

At www.packt.com, you can also read a collection of free technical articles, sign up for a range of free newsletters, and receive exclusive discounts and offers on Packt books and eBooks.

Other Books You May Enjoy

If you enjoyed this book, you may be interested in these other books by Packt:

Python Microservices Development – 2nd edition

Tarek Ziadé

ISBN: 978-1-80107-630-2

- Explore what microservices are and how to design them
- Configure and package your code according to modern best practices
- Identify a component of a larger service that can be turned into a microservice
- Handle more incoming requests, more effectively
- Protect your application with a proxy or firewall
- Use Kubernetes and containers to deploy a microservice
- Make changes to an API provided by a microservice safely and keep things working
- Identify the factors to look for to get started with an unfamiliar cloud provider

Python Web Development with Sanic

Adam Hopkins

ISBN: 978-1-80181-441-6

- Understand the difference between WSGI, Async, and ASGI servers

- Discover how Sanic organizes incoming data, why it does it, and how to make the most of it

- Implement best practices for building reliable, performant, and secure web apps

- Explore useful techniques for successfully testing and deploying a Sanic web app

- Create effective solutions for the modern web, including task management, bot integration, and GraphQL

- Identify security concerns and understand how to deal with them in your Sanic apps

Packt is searching for authors like you

If you're interested in becoming an author for Packt, please visit `authors.packtpub.com` and apply today. We have worked with thousands of developers and tech professionals, just like you, to help them share their insight with the global tech community. You can make a general application, apply for a specific hot topic that we are recruiting an author for, or submit your own idea.

Share Your Thoughts

Now you've finished *Django 4 for the Impatient*, we'd love to hear your thoughts! Scan the QR code below to go straight to the Amazon review page for this book and share your feedback or leave a review on the site that you purchased it from.

https://packt.link/r/1803245832

Your review is important to us and the tech community and will help us make sure we're delivering excellent quality content.